GOYA
a pictorial biography

GOYA
a pictorial biography

BY VYVYAN HOLLAND

A STUDIO BOOK
THE VIKING PRESS · NEW YORK

To MARGARET RAWLINGS in affection and admiration

© *Vyvyan Holland 1961*
Published in 1961 by The Viking Press, Inc.
625 Madison Avenue, New York 22, N.Y.
Library of Congress catalog card number 61–15436
Printed in Great Britain by Clarke and Sherwell Ltd Northampton and
Jarrold and Sons Ltd Norwich

Saragossa, on the River Ebro

TWO OF THE GREATEST PAINTERS OF ALL TIME have been Spaniards:
Velazquez and Goya, each supreme in his own way. It might be argued that
three others should be added: Murillo, El Greco, and Picasso. But Murillo, for
all his craftsmanship, too often yielded to sentiment; El Greco, although most
of his painting was done in Spain, was a Cretan who learned his art in Venice
and Rome and did not come to Spain until he was about thirty years of age;
and Picasso is perhaps a little too close to us for a definitive assessment of his
work to be made. Velazquez may have been a greater painter than Goya, but
Goya was undoubtedly the more prolific and the more varied in his choice of
subjects and in the media in which he worked, being equally at home with
the pencil, the brush, and the tools of the engraver and lithographer.

Unlike many artists who live self-centred lives and hold themselves aloof
from the world, Goya was a gregarious man who took an intense interest in
people and in their everyday lives, their joys, and their sorrows. So, to appreciate
Goya's work and to understand the way in which it developed, it must be
related to the turbulent times in which he lived. A. de Beruete, the eminent
historian of Spanish painting, summed up Goya's work in these words:

'He was an essentially Spanish genius whose work is a mirror in which is
reflected, in faithful and permanent form, the whole social history of a period,

5

embracing all strata of society from kings to beggars, and giving us an exact feeling of something which otherwise we could only have visualised in a vague and confused manner. And he expressed it with that clarity and sincerity which characterises all Spanish artistic production.'

All the changes brought about by political intrigue, insurrection, and war are paraded before us in his work; no other artist, with the exception of Hogarth, has left such a complete record of the times in which he lived.

In writing the story of Goya's life, or indeed of the life of almost any artist, one is immediately confronted with the difficulty of placing events in their right chronological order and of giving them their right dates. Other famous men lead lives which are easily traced and documented, but the artist's fame lies mainly in his pictures, and these, even if they are signed, which is by no means always the case, are more often than not undated. Luckily for us, Goya was an industrious correspondent, and a large number of his letters have been preserved, a fact which is all-important in fixing the dates of the principal events in his life. Some of his earlier biographers floundered badly in this respect, but now the picture has become clear.

Parents Goya's full name was Francisco José Goya y Lucientes. His father's name was José Goya, but in Spain a child always adds the name of his mother to that of his father, and Francisco's mother was named Engracia Lucientes. This peculiarity is an important fact to bear in mind in dealing with Spanish biography, although the two names are only used on formal occasions, in addressing letters, etc.; in practice, only the father's name is used, as in other European countries. The elder Goya was the son of a notary in Saragossa, but the family seems to have suffered a decline, as José himself became a working gilder in Saragossa, a distinct descent in the social scale. Nevertheless, he married rather above his station, his wife Engracia being of *hidalgo* parentage.

At that time there were about half a million *hidalgos* in Spain—roughly five per cent of the population. The word is a contraction of *hijo de algo*—the son of somebody—and to these petty nobles work was something that was degrading and to be avoided at all costs. This naturally led to a great deal of misery among the impoverished upper classes, and King Charles III tried to remedy it by issuing a decree to the effect that the trade of tailor, shoemaker, or carpenter did not in any way degrade either the family or the person who practised it. The decree was dated 1783; unfortunately, the French Revolution, with its ideas of equality, struck terror into the hearts of the Spanish rulers, and in 1803 the decree was virtually rescinded by a new royal order to the effect that there was never any intention of raising manual labourers to the upper classes. Incidentally, later in life Goya inserted a 'de' before his name, pretending to be of noble descent through his mother.

Goya was born in this house in the little village of Fuendetodos near Saragossa

Engracia brought as her dowry a small property near the village of Fuende-todos, not far from the city of Saragossa, the capital of the ancient Kingdom of Aragon. Whereupon José Goya abandoned his work as a gilder and set about the business of becoming a landed proprietor; in point of fact, he became a sort of peasant farmer, tilling the land himself. It was in the village of Fuendetodos that Francisco Goya was born, in his father's house, No. 18 Calle de Alfóndiga, on March 30, 1746, a few months before the death of the reigning monarch King Philip V. But the farming venture seems not to have prospered; three years later, we find the family established in Saragossa itself, in the Calle de la Morería Cerrada (literally, the Street of the Forbidden Moorish Quarter), with

Saragossa: the Cathedral of El Pilar

José Goya back at his old trade of gilding. He was more successful at this than he had been as a farmer, as is shown by the fact that he soon came to own this new house and managed to educate his children by his labours. Francisco was one of three sons. The others were Camillo, who became a priest, and Tomás, who followed his father's profession of gilder; there was also a daughter, who died in her thirties. José sold his house in 1780, probably to pay for the completion of his children's education.

Goya's schooldays   Young Francisco passed his early youth between Fuendetodos and Saragossa and received an elementary education at the hands of the priesthood; he learned to read and write and was inculcated with a great deal of religion, but there the matter ended; like most people in eighteenth-century Spain he never learned to

Martin Zapater, Goya's lifelong friend

spell properly. One of his school-friends was Martin Zapater, with whom he kept up a voluminous correspondence extending over nearly forty years. Though Zapater's own letters have disappeared, all Goya's letters to him are still in existence and they show that Zapater exercised a restraining influence on Goya and gave him good advice which he frequently followed.

Whatever the shortcomings of Goya's education, he very early showed an interest in art, and his aptitude in that direction soon attracted the notice of the Church. Eventually, Don Felice Salzedo, the Prior of a Carthusian monastery on the outskirts of Saragossa, was so impressed with the young artist's work that he brought it to the notice of the head of the Pignatelli family, the Conde de Fuentes, who was the quasi-feudal overlord of Fuendetodos and of all the

Interest in art

9

A street scene in Saragossa
with its 'leaning' tower

district surrounding it. Don Felice's recommendation roused the Count's interest to such an extent that he had the young man placed under the instruction of one José Luzan y Martinez, who was the foremost art teacher in Saragossa at the time.

Goya's first teacher   Luzan was born in Saragossa in 1710, and he, too, owed his training to the patronage of the Pignatellis. He had a wide knowledge of European art, having, as a student, travelled all over France and Italy to study the works of the great masters. This was essential for any aspiring painter who wished to acquire a knowledge of the world's art. Today, there are such excellent reproductions of all the great pictures that they can be studied and absorbed at home; but in the eighteenth century there were no such facilities, and travel was the only way of studying. Alas for fame! No modern art lover would ever have heard of Luzan if he had not been Goya's first teacher; there is no example of his work in the Prado in Madrid. His is a reflected glory deriving from the works of his most famous pupil.

The Cathedral of La Seo in Saragossa

Interested though he was in his art, Goya was always essentially a lover of life and of all that it could provide for him in the way of excitement, adventure, and romance; so it was not long before stories began to circulate about the escapades of the young student. He occupied certain of his leisure hours in becoming quite a passable musician, no doubt so as to ingratiate himself with the young ladies. And, in case this might lead to differences of opinion with young men with similar ideas, he became an expert swordsman, an accomplishment which it was very advisable for a young man to acquire in those days, especially if he had romantic leanings.

Curiously enough, Goya's first major brush with authority came about through religious enthusiasm. There were two cathedrals in Saragossa, that of La Seo and that of El Pilar; considerable rivalry existed between the two as to which was the more important. Periodical processions were held in which the images of the patron saints of their respective cathedrals were carried through the streets, accompanied by bands of young men; this frequently led to fights

The 'curtains' above the altarpiece in the parish church at Fuendetodos

between the rival factions, sometimes even ending in slaughter. This hardly seems to be in accordance with Christian principles, but we must remember that the Holy Office of the Inquisition was in full power at the time, and religion in Spain was apt to be a very violent affair indeed. Goya, in spite of his youth, was one of the chief instigators of these encounters, and matters reached a pitch at which he began to attract the curiosity of the Inquisition itself; so in 1765 he left Saragossa, either to escape the attentions of the Holy Office or, which is more likely, to get on in the world. Whatever the reason, we next find him in Madrid.

What a pity it is that the early scribblings of great painters are so seldom preserved. Fond parents may occasionally, for sentimental reasons, store away their very young offspring's attempts at drawing people and animals, but how many drawings survive which were made by the great masters in their art-classes? Nothing of Goya's early work has been preserved, except an altarpiece in Fuendetodos, painted when he was still a pupil of Luzan's. Nearly fifty years later he looked at it again and, turning to Martin Zapater, who was with him, he shook his head and said: 'I don't believe I ever painted that!'

Madrid in 1765

By Spanish standards Madrid is a comparatively modern city. When, after the
ejection of the Moors, Spaniards decided to form a united country, the question
arose as to where the capital of this new country was to be. There was, quite
naturally, jealousy among the old Kingdoms. The North would not accept
Seville or Granada, and the South was equally set against Saragossa, Leon, or
Toledo. To break this deadlock it was decided to create an entirely new capital
and to develop the small town of Madrid, on the River Manzanares. Madrid
does not, as most people believe, derive its name from *madre*, as being the mother
city of Spain, but from its old Moorish name *Majerit*; it was originally a fortress
outpost of Toledo. The choice of the site was influenced largely by Charles V,
who thought that the air blowing down from the Guadarrama mountains
would suit his gout.

Goya was nineteen years of age when he first went to Madrid and, in the
words of one of his biographers, had developed from a sad-faced child 'into a

An early self-portrait
by Goya

bold-tempered and strongly built youth, who looked the world in the face
without fear, and possessed an undeniable gift of personal attraction'. That very
gift of personal attraction was to lead him into a great deal of trouble in the
course of his life, but it was trouble that had its romantic compensations.

Although his development was rather slow, Goya did not neglect his artistic
education in Madrid. His first step was to try to become a pupil of the Academy
of San Fernando. This institution which, with the King's painters, controlled
the art world of Spain, had been founded in 1752, during the reign of King
Ferdinand VI, after whom it was named. It was essential for the aspiring
painter to be connected with it, and the first step was to become a pupil of its
school. The procedure for gaining admission to the school was a complicated
one; there were many applicants and the number of pupils was strictly limited.
First, the candidate was required to submit to the Committee of Academicians
a painting on a subject selected by the Academy. If the candidate's picture met
with approval he was allowed to enter a competition for any vacancy there
might be. The subject selected for 1766, when Goya first arrived in Madrid,
was: 'Martha, Empress of Constantinople, presents herself to King Alfonso the
Wise at Burgos and asks him for one third of the sum which the Sultan of
Egypt had set as the ransom of the Emperor Baldwin, her husband. The
Spanish monarch orders the entire sum to be given to her.'

*The Apparition of the
Virgin of the Pillar*,
Goya's painting in the parish
church of his native village

Goya's painting has long since disappeared, but it must have satisfied the
Academicians, as he was allowed to enter the competition proper, with seven
other candidates. This entailed painting a picture there and then on an assigned
subject, two hours being allowed for the work. The subject on this occasion
was: 'Within sight of the Spanish army in Italy, Juan de Urbina and Diego
de Parades discuss which of the two should be given the arms of the Marchese
di Pescara.' When the result of the competition was announced, Goya's name
was not among the first three. This must have been a disappointment to him,
but his attempt stood him in good stead, because it brought him into contact
with Francisco Bayeu y Subias, one of the official Court Painters and the
principal judge of the competition. Goya entered Bayeu's studio as a pupil and
through him he came under the tutelage of Anton Raphael Mengs, the First
Painter to the Spanish Court.

He meets Bayeu

15

Mengs, the First Court Painter
to Charles III

Mengs was born in 1728 at Aussig in Bohemia, the son of Ismael Me⌐
the Dresden Court Painter. After various vicissitudes he came to Spain, eve
tually becoming virtual dictator of art there. His work, like that of many
another painter of his generation, suffered from the conviction, implanted when
he was a young student in Rome, that to be a great painter one must slavishly
follow the works of antiquity. He was dominated by the ideals of Raphael,
Correggio, and Winckelmann, upon whose art he modelled his own and from
whose influence he could never escape. He died in 1779, but not before he had
started Goya well upon his career. Little is known of the personal relationship
between the two men, but there must have been a firm and loyal friendship
between master and pupil, and it was certainly to Mengs that Goya owed most
of his early success; it says a great deal for Goya's strength of mind and his
independent spirit that he was not permanently influenced by Mengs's teaching.

A street in Madrid, drawn by Goya

This does not mean that Goya rejected the great painters of the past. Indeed, thanks to the patronage of Bayeu, he was able to spend a great deal of time studying the paintings in the various royal collections. Today this is a simple matter, for practically all the art treasures that belonged to the Royal Family are housed in the Prado in Madrid. But in Goya's time they were distributed throughout the royal palaces, and to see them he had to do a great deal of travelling by very uncomfortable transport. They were concealed in Toledo, Aranjuez, the Escorial, and other royal residences, and few people had any knowledge of them or opportunity of seeing them. In these collections Goya could study the works of Hieronymus Bosch and Pieter Bruegel, which were to influence his etchings so much in later life. Teniers also made a deep impression upon him, as well as Tintoretto, Titian, and Veronese, but this did not result in slavish imitation; Goya absorbed just as much as he wanted from them and no more.

Early influences

Murillo, who influenced all young Spanish painters of the period, was an important influence on Goya, but his ideal was the great Velazquez. Oddly enough, Velazquez was not held in very high esteem in Europe at the end of

17

▲ The Escorial, in the mountains near Madrid   The Royal Palace at Aranjuez, near Madrid ▼

The Duel

the eighteenth century, when the accent was on the more light-hearted works of Fragonard, Boucher, Lancret, and Pater; but Goya clearly rejected these as being playthings for the French Court and aristocracy, and continued to develop along his own lines.

Goya's life in Madrid was full of incident. The story that he was found in the street with a dagger in his back, after an amorous adventure and a tiff with a rival, has been told too often to be rejected as a legend, particularly as it seems to have resulted in his precipitate flight from Madrid to Rome in 1769. He himself certainly never denied the story. But in fact in the eighteenth century every artist who could afford to do so went to Italy to study Renaissance paintings.

The fugitive had no money to finance his journey to Italy and none to live upon when he got there. The journey overland through France was a long, tiresome, and expensive one, so he made his way from Madrid to the South of Spain as a member of a company of bull-fighters who travelled from village to village to exhibit their skill. The truth of this is confirmed by his great friend

The square in front of St Peter's in Rome at the time Goya visited the city in 1769

in later life, the poet and dramatist Leandro Fernández de Moratín who, in a letter of 1825, wrote: 'Goya says that in his time he has been a bull-fighter and that with the sword in his hand he fears no man.' The word Moratín uses for 'sword' is *estoque*, which is particularly applied to the weapon with which the bull is dispatched in the ring. And from any southern Spanish port it would have been an easy matter to work a passage in a ship bound for Italy.

Rome   Goya's arrival in Rome coincided with a number of the frequent festivities for which the Eternal City was famous in the eighteenth century. Shortly after his arrival, celebrations and processions were taking place in honour of the newly elected Pope, Clement XIV. It was also carnival time, and there were constant parades in which ladies of the most ancient and aristocratic families in Rome displayed their scantily concealed charms and were bombarded by the populace with small bunches of primroses and violets, as they passed by in their wagons. All this pageantry and romance appealed strongly to Goya's ardent nature; and what could excite his imagination more than the sight of the Pope astride a prancing white gelding, preceded by the pontifical cross, surrounded by all the magnificence of the Papal Court and escorted by the Swiss Guard with their bright-coloured breeches and useless armour? He must have been in

A street-scene in
eighteenth-century Rome

his element, the more so as he was, even at that time, not particularly drawn to
the Church. And the anticlimax to the carnival must also have appealed to his
sprightly mind. For, as one contemporary observer puts it, 'on Ash Wednesday,
the ladies who had flaunted their charms so blatantly in the public gaze as
Venus or Phryne crept modestly to Mass, heavily draped in black, afterwards
confessing the sins which they had enjoyed so much an hour or two before'.

It is generally supposed that Goya's father, José, sold some of his property
to enable his son to pursue his studies in Rome, for he had no Government
subsidy. In one respect this was fortunate for Goya, as he was not bound down
by the rules and regulations which applied to most of the other Spanish students.
On the contrary, he spent his time studying rather than producing; but, to
quote one of his earliest biographers, Goya, being a genius, was busiest when
least active. He painted scenes of Spanish life and sold them to visitors to
Rome; there are probably dozens of these hanging unrecognized on walls all
over Europe. He even attracted the notice of the Russian Ambassador, who

asked him to go to St Petersburg to assist in a scheme of the Empress Catherine II for starting a modern school of art there. He declined; the thought of the Russian winter was altogether too much for his sunny southern nature.

Goya's escapades Many are the stories told of Goya's adventures and foolhardiness during his two years in Rome. They cannot all be apocryphal. On one occasion he is credited with having climbed the lantern of the dome of St Peter's to carve his name upon a stone which had been untouched by human hand since it was put in place. He had heard that Poussin had tried to do the same thing and he decided that what a Frenchman could do, a Spaniard could do better. Goya is also supposed to have met and associated there with the French painter Jacques Louis David. Unfortunately all the stories of their friendship must be summarily dismissed, because Goya left Rome in 1771 and David did not go there until 1775, after he had won the Prix de Rome in Paris.

Quarrelling, gambling, and love-making seem to have been the main occupations of the young men in Rome at that time, particularly the students and artists. There was little order in the city; robberies and murders were of nightly, and even daily occurrence. In the disordered state of Europe, the most violent political intrigue went on unchecked and assassinations were carried out by the orders of princes, cardinals, and even ambassadors; no peace-loving citizen would venture through the streets at night without a heavily armed guard. This state of affairs suited Francisco Goya, to whom a brawl, either with fists or with knives, was just a pleasant interlude in the course of daily life.

Things finally came to a head when one dark night he burgled a convent with the object of abducting a novice who had taken his fancy. There is no doubt of the truth of this story, though there is no record of the names of either the nun or her convent. What is known is the fact that he was caught red-handed and flung into prison. This was a very serious matter, as the penalty for violating a convent was death without hope of reprieve. Goya had, luckily for him, many influential friends among the Spanish colony in Rome, and the Spanish Ambassador came to his aid, interceding with the Holy Father on his behalf, with the result that he was pardoned, but expelled from the Papal States with ignominy.

He made his way back to Spain through northern Italy and France, painting as he went, and selling his pictures in order to live. He was fairly successful in this, as can be gathered from the following description of a prize distribution at the Royal Academy of Fine Arts in Parma that appeared in the *Moniteur de la France* in January 1772: 'The second prize for painting was awarded to Monsieur François Goya, a pupil of señor Vajeu [*sic*], Court Painter to the King of Spain. If Monsieur Goya had been more robust in his composition, he would probably have shared the first prize.'

La Fé, a detail of one of the frescoes which Goya painted in the Cathedral of
El Pilar in Saragossa

We next hear of him being commissioned to take part in the decoration of
the Cathedral of El Pilar in Saragossa, the building of which was begun in
1684. Originally designed by the architect Herrera, the plans were later
drastically altered by Rodriguez Ventura. The final result leaves much to be
desired; it has been rather sarcastically described as 'one of the purest examples
of the Louis XVI style'. Be that as it may, the main structure was completed in
1771 and the time had come for the interior decoration to be considered.

*First important
commission*

It is a little surprising that in spite of Goya's recent escapade, news of which
would certainly have preceded him, he was asked to submit designs for this
project. The Committee of Approval consisted largely of priests, who took a
rather poor view of Goya's somewhat irregular mode of life. He had already
been expelled, or practically expelled, from Saragossa for bad behaviour; his
departures from Madrid and Rome had been equally precipitate, and the fumes

The Adoration of the Name of the Lord in the Cathedral of El Pilar; a fresco by Goya

of his romantic encounters were still whirling around his head. But Art overcame Morality, and in any case Goya had two very powerful and influential sponsors in Luzan and Bayeu, particularly Bayeu, with whom he was at the moment on the most intimate terms and whose sister he subsequently married. There was, however, considerable difference of opinion over the sketches that he submitted, and the acceptance of his designs was largely due to the insistence of an aged and liberal-minded canon, Don Mathias Allué. In January 1772, then, Goya received the commission to paint the frescoes, and so quickly did he work that they were finished by June 1 of the same year.

The Saragossa frescoes

The result is far from being a credit to Goya. In the first place, the position of the frescoes is unfortunate, the vault of the cathedral being too high and its

Goya's Holy Family

lighting too dim for them to be seen clearly. Were they not by Goya, no one would ever notice them, for they are no better than other frescoes painted in other parts of the cathedral. In fact, they were hack work; his heart was not in them. This, too, was the period when Goya's work was least satisfactory: before he had found his own feet, when he was temporarily influenced by El Greco and was inclined to go in for pastel shades and to exaggerate corners, cornices, and the deep shadows thrown by the midday sun.

During the following three years Francisco was almost entirely engaged in Church work, which came to him as the result of his part in the decoration of the Saragossa Cathedral. His outstanding work at this time was his decorations for the Charterhouse of Aula Dei. These took him, on and off, about two

The *Desposorros Virgen*, one of the murals Goya painted in the Charterhouse of the Aula Dei, near Saragossa

years. They comprised eleven large compositions, some of which were fifteen feet wide and others more than thirty. This was an important undertaking for a painter who thus far had nothing to his credit but a few rather nebulous frescoes on a cathedral ceiling. But he was extremely happy in his work there, because the monks were too occupied with their own concerns to interfere with his. Unfortunately, nearly all the work he did there was destroyed during the French occupation of Spain at the beginning of the nineteenth century.

It was at this time, too, that he painted his *Holy Family*—a very beautiful interpretation. Most of the deeply religious painters, such as Murillo and El Greco, etherealize the Virgin Mary and depict her as a woman without any human emotions whatever, except when she is shown sorrowing at the foot of the Cross with the dead Christ in her lap—the so-called *Pietà*. Goya, on the other hand, not being very religious himself, makes her a devoted wife and a lovely mother who is completely absorbed in her family; his picture is just

The Crucifixion by Goya ▶

Detail of a portrait of Goya's
teacher and later brother-in-law
Francisco Bayeu

a natural group of happy human beings. It is believed that the picture of
the Madonna was inspired by his future wife, Josefa Bayeu. From the same
period, also, comes his *Crucifixion*, now in the Prado, in which Our Lord's
feet are shown supported by a block of wood, which is much more convincing
than the conventional treatment, in which His feet are shown nailed to the
wood of the Cross, in a position that could not possibly have been maintained
unless He had been levitated in some way.

In March 1775 Goya married Josefa, the sister of his old teacher and patron. *Marriage*
His portrait of her in the Prado does not show her as a particularly handsome
woman, though she is said to have had remarkably beautiful red hair. Doubts
have from time to time been expressed as to whether this portrait, which is
certainly by Goya, really is that of Josefa; but a comparison of the lady's features
in the portrait with those of Francisco Bayeu in Goya's painting of him dispels
any doubt about the matter.

◀ *Josefa Bayeu*, who became Goya's wife in 1775

The moment of truth: a scene from a bull-fight as etched by Goya

The young couple set up house in Madrid at No. 66 Carrera de San Gerónimo, and for a time Francisco Goya gave up his wild ways, his perpetual quest for adventure, and his bad companions, of whom he had many, and tried to apply himself, within the limits of his fiery temperament, to the task of becoming a model husband and father. But he could not be expected to abandon for ever all his normal habits and activities, merely by reason of having acquired a wedding-ring. He was a devotee of bull-fighting and had many friends in the fraternity, as his *Tauromaquia* paintings and engravings and his portraits of popular bull-fighters show us. By his very nature he was always attracted to the more adventurous members of the community who lived by their wits or by their physique or who, like the gipsies, were outcasts from

José Romero was one
of the most famous
bull-fighters of Spain

respectable society. He felt at home with the gipsies, with the young men who
spent their nights gambling, playing guitars, and chanting *jotas* to their lady-
loves, and also with the dancing girls whose deep brown eyes and brilliant teeth
drew him as snakes will draw a bird.

Much as Goya loved his wife, he could not avert his gaze from any beauty
who happened to flash her eyes at him. Whatever his contemporaries may have
said in disparagement of him, one thing remains abundantly clear: he was
attractive to women. At this time, he was rapidly ingratiating himself into the
high society of the land, and the ladies of the Court began to find in him not
only a painter who flattered their vanity, but an agreeable companion and a
gentleman of parts.

In *The Stilt-walkers* Goya catches all the gaiety of his subject

first mention of Goya in connexion with the tapestries was in June 1776, and he delivered his initial design at the end of October of that year. During the following four years he devoted most of his time to this work. By January 1778 he had produced a further ten, and seven more by April. These cartoons brought him immediate recognition among all classes, particularly among the ordinary people. The old King, Charles III, indicated that he wanted the tapestries to deal with the daily life of Spain and not with Court life or mythology, which Goya, left to himself, would very likely have chosen. The cartoon designs are among the best known of his paintings; he is credited with having made forty-six, of which thirty-eight are now in the Prado, and one is in Edinburgh. It is impossible to date any of them with precision, though it is known that *La Merienda*, representing a picnic on the banks of the Manzanares, was the first to be delivered and was therefore painted towards the end of 1776.

The Crockery Seller, a study in contrasts between upper- and lower-class life in Madrid

Among the best of them, in addition to *La Merienda*, are *La Vendimia* ('The Vintage'), *La Gallina Ciega* ('Blind Man's Buff'), *Los Zancos* ('The Stilt-walkers'), and *El Cacharrero* ('The Crockery Seller'). To appreciate them fully, the finished tapestries in the Escorial must be seen, as they show how well Goya understood the quality of the medium for which they were designed.

While he was engaged on these tapestry cartoons, Francisco was also accept- *Begins etching* ing commissions for portraits and experimenting with etching, which he had recently taken up. His earliest known etching is *The Flight into Egypt*, executed in 1775. Oddly enough, though Goya's etchings are not by any means his best work, they are probably the work with which his name is most frequently connected. This is the case with a great many artists, probably because an etching or an engraving is more lasting than a drawing and is so much more easily stored than a large canvas. As one of Goya's biographers

Don Juan Antonio Cuervo,
Director of the
Royal Academy of San Fernando

puts it: 'Modern artists, with a few notable exceptions, seem afraid to etch. If the rank and file seek for immortality, let them start at once. Their pictures may be forgotten, but their etchings will wander from portfolio to portfolio for eternity.'

In 1779, while still at work on the cartoons, he applied for a position as a Court Painter, but, to his disappointment and indignation, the application was refused. He was, however, consoled for this set-back to his ambitions by being *Elected to* elected to the Royal Academy of San Fernando. Forty years later, as the most *the Academy* distinguished member of the Academy, he was to paint a portrait of its Director, then Don Juan Antonio Cuervo.

Goya was now living more or less permanently in Madrid. Nevertheless, as an Aragonese his heart was always in Aragon, particularly in its capital city, Saragossa, where he had spent most of his childhood and with which he kept constantly in touch through his correspondence with his boyhood friend

The Avenue of the Prado, a favourite meeting-place for Madrid high society

Martin Zapater, until the latter's death in the early years of the nineteenth century; poor Francisco was, indeed, to outlive all his contemporaries. But to return to Madrid; his life there was divided between his home, his friends among the populace, and his sitters among the Spanish aristocracy. He hated cant, hypocrisy and all forms of law, rule and restraint that were likely to interfere with his pleasures. And at the same time he moved in the highest Court circles, though here, too, behaviour was becoming increasingly lax with the gradually diminishing authority of the ageing Charles III and the consequent domination of the Court by Maria Luisa of Parma, the wife of the heir to the throne and a lady whose mode of life was most unconventional.

Court circles

To understand the peculiar position in which Goya found himself it is necessary to get a general idea of the Spanish Court in those days. King Charles III was an old man who took little interest in anything but the salvation of his soul, an ambition based largely upon the rigours of the Holy Office of the Inquisition.

Mengs's *Portrait of
Maria Luisa* before
she became Queen

Maria Luisa, his daughter-in-law, was a woman of coarse habits and violent
passions who was neglected by her husband, the future Charles IV, who himself cared for nothing but hunting. Maria Luisa ruled the Court with the help
of her favourite and lover, Manuel de Godoy, who befriended Francisco Goya
and became his powerful ally.

It might not be out of place here to stress the fact that much of Goya's
greatness lies in the fact that he was not a religious painter. With few exceptions,
Spanish artists concentrated largely on religious subjects, alternating, as a
relief, with others of a classical or mythological nature. Goya, on the other
hand, was essentially a lay artist, delighting in recording the everyday happen-
ings taking place around him and taking more pleasure in painting a pretty
face than a saintly one. He never tried to idealize anyone, neither his own wife
nor his Queen, but painted them exactly as he saw them; in fact, he may be

Goya's *Portrait of Maria Luisa* Queen of Spain and wife of Charles IV ▶

One of Goya's earliest etchings—a copy of a Velazquez painting

said to have been the initiator of the realistic style of painting, upon which the Romantic school in Europe was based. Hugh Stokes, in his biography of Goya, sums it up thus:

'Goya lacked the spirituality of the old Spanish masters. They were mystics, surrounded by an invisible world. Goya could not escape the inherited tendencies of untold centuries. Aragon is a land of soothsayers and witches. He fought against superstitions which he could not wholly reject. He turned his back on Heaven, and was haunted by Hell. There is no celestial peace in anything he produced.'

It was in 1775 that Goya began to etch. His early efforts were mostly copies of Velazquez and other artists and are not of any real importance; indeed, Goya

The Flagellants, an example of the religious hysteria that was still rife in Goya's Spain

himself destroyed most of them. The fact is that he was still experimenting in this medium, and the etchings for which he is famous were not produced until many years later.

Goya revisited Saragossa whenever the opportunity arose. His name is now honoured there above all others, but during his lifetime his fellow-citizens seemed to have treated him with little less than contempt. The lukewarmness of his religious feelings may have had something to do with this, since Saragossa was a very religious city, ruled largely, as were all Spanish provincial towns at that time, by the priesthood and the Inquisition. After his initial commission to paint the frescoes in the Cathedral of El Pilar, he was given no more work there for some time, though this was not for lack of trying. He had to wait until 1780 for his next chance to decorate the cathedral. When it came, he wrote to his faithful friend Zapater asking him to find him somewhere to live and to furnish it with a table, five chairs, some kitchen and eating utensils, an oil-lamp, a violin, and a draught-board complete with men.

The violin is rather a peculiar request. One would have thought that a violin-player would have liked to choose his instrument himself—but such impulsiveness is typical of Goya; he hated ostentation, and he hated being cluttered up with useless possessions.

To quote Hugh Stokes again:

'Goya was a terrific worker, and he earned large sums of money, but he sought recreation outside the practice of his art. When the leisure hour came, he did not meditatively dream through a portfolio, or argue with a friend over the merits of a canvas. Instead, he threw himself into fresh action, dived into the pot-houses of Madrid, crossed foils with the latest *maître d'épée* from Paris or Rome, sought an adventure in the groves of the Prado, spent scented hours in an aristocratic boudoir, or fraternised with the gipsies who camped on the outskirts of the town. Goya was essentially a man of action.'

Quarrel with
Bayeu Although negotiations for Francisco to resume the work on the cathedral had begun in 1774, it was not until 1780 that he started the new work. In that year he appears to have been engaged on the frescoes, or at least the sketches for them, working with his younger brother-in-law, Ramon Bayeu. It was, however, Francisco Bayeu who was really in charge of the operation, and this naturally annoyed Goya, who was growing tired of the perpetual domination of his brother-in-law, whom he regarded as an inferior artist to himself. He had not recovered from the blow to his pride caused by the refusal to appoint him a Court Painter, a set-back which he probably attributed, with some reason, to Francisco Bayeu's jealousy. And now Goya found himself in a position in which he was more or less under Bayeu's orders. Bitter recriminations ensued, in which the Committee charged with the cathedral decorations found themselves in utter confusion. Bayeu complained of Goya's insubordination and lack of co-ordination with his ideas, and the Committee, being a collection of prominent citizens and priests, without any pretension to artistic knowledge, supported Bayeu against Goya, since Bayeu was a Court Painter and an older man. The situation was summarized in the report issued by the Committee:

'The Committee, taking into account the fact that Goya had come to paint owing, in large measure, to the influence and praise of his brother-in-law Bayeu, agreed that Canon Allué, the director of the building operations, should carefully supervise the artist and his work and should make such criticisms as he thought might be necessary. He should also make it clear to Goya how grateful he should be to Don Francisco Bayeu for appointing him to be his assistant.'

The Virgin as Queen of the Martyrs—a sketch for Goya's frescoes in the Cathedral of El Pilar

Saragossa, the city with two cathedrals

Nothing could have been more calculated to infuriate Goya. In the result, he made no attempt to harmonize his own frescoes with those of the brothers Bayeu, and the best that can be said of his work in the Cathedral of El Pilar is that it is disappointing.

The whole quarrel came to a head in a letter written by Goya to the Cathedral Committee from Saragossa on March 17, 1781. In it he accuses Bayeu of malice and declares that he has had to put up with calumny, insults, and contempt at his hands. He complains that he was told that some of the figures in the decoration of the dome would have to be altered, and that steps had been taken to see that this was done by some 'dauber' to be chosen apparently at random.

Canon Allué was getting tired of these family squabbles and delegated Father Salzedo to try to mediate. Father Salzedo was the priest who first persuaded Goya to concentrate on his art; he was one of the few people to whose advice Goya would ever listen, and through his mediation the bad feeling between Goya and Bayeu was temporarily allayed. Goya wrote a letter to Canon Allué in which he agreed to collaborate with Bayeu in the preparation of a fresh set of designs and apologized for his irritability. This peaceful pact was, unfortunately, of short duration and a fresh quarrel broke out between Bayeu and Goya, who declared himself to have been insulted again. Goya asked

Another Goya sketch for the frescoes in the Cathedral of El Pilar

permission to leave the work and to return to Madrid; this angered the Committee, which considered, with some reason, that it had put up with enough,
and a letter was sent to Goya which did nothing to abate the storm. It stated
emphatically that in no circumstances would he be allowed to continue his
work in the cathedral, but that the Director (Canon Allué) proposed to honour
Goya's wife—as the sister of Francisco Bayeu, who had done so much skilful
work in the decoration of the cathedral—with a decoration. On receipt of this
letter Goya immediately left Saragossa, and returned to Madrid, where he
arrived towards the end of June.

Various reasons have been advanced to account for the feud between Goya
and his brother-in-law, but the most likely one is that Bayeu was jealous of the
mounting reputation of one whom he had always regarded as a promising pupil
and who was now becoming a serious rival. It has also been suggested that
Bayeu was furious with the way Goya treated his sister, Josefa, by his frequent
infidelities, although Josefa herself always bore such lapses with fortitude.

Soon after the quarrel between Goya and his brother-in-law over the Pilar
decorations, José Goya, Francisco's father, died in December 1781, intestate *Father dies*
because he had nothing to leave. His widow left Saragossa to join her son in
Madrid, but Spanish women are more attached to places than to people, and

45

The Puerta del Sol, then as now the very heart of Madrid

she fretted for her old haunts and very soon returned to Saragossa, where she remained until her death, supported by an annunity provided by her artist son.

Francisco took his father's death very much to heart. There was genuine affection between them, a fact that makes it all the more strange that the son never painted a portrait of the father. Indeed, very few portraits of any of Goya's family have come down to us from his brush. There is in Berlin a portrait believed to be of his mother, and there is the portrait of his wife which has already been mentioned. There is also one of his sister and one of a daughter-in-law, both of which are in private collections. Perhaps, like surgeons who refuse to operate upon members of their own family, he avoided painting them for fear that he would not be able to do them justice.

His differences of opinion with the cathedral authorities of Saragossa, which led to his abrupt return to Madrid, were really all to the good, as there was a great deal of work for an artist to do in Madrid at that time. The building of the Church of San Francisco el Grande was nearly completed. There were seven altars, each one of which would need a painting to adorn it, and on Goya's return he was immediately commissioned to execute one of them, in spite of opposition from the Court painting clique, which frowned on his disregard of the rigid conventions to which they adhered. However, the Count

Portrait of an Old Lady, the sitter may have been Goya's mother

The Infante Don Luis,
brother of Charles III
(detail of the portrait)

After his success in San Francisco el Grande, work crowded in upon Goya *Success* and he was kept hard at it, though he was handicapped by a nervous ailment which had first attacked him in 1780 and which was to cause him acute discomfort for the next ten years. He painted several subjects of a devotional character for a religious college in Salamanca, and, largely again through the influence of Floridablanca, he began to be overwhelmed with commissions to paint portraits of personages in Court circles. Among these were the Infante Don Luis, younger brother of Charles III, with whom he soon became on terms of the greatest friendship; he was invited to the Infante's palace of Arenas de San Pedro in Avila, and there, in intervals between going on hunting expeditions with his host, he painted portraits of the Prince, his beautiful wife Maria Teresa Vallabriga, and their children. Altogether, Goya painted about a dozen portraits of this family, half of which were of Maria Teresa.

◀ *Charles III in hunting costume*

Don Luis's marriage to Maria Teresa had been frowned on by the Court because, although of a noble Aragonese family, she was not of the Royal Blood. So the Prince spent much of his time at Arenas, living the life of a private gentleman, hunting and patronizing the Arts. He died in August 1785, and after his death his widow was forbidden to live in Madrid or any of the provincial capitals. Her children, however, fared much better; of her two daughters one married Manuel de Godoy and the other the Duke of San Fernando, whilst her son became Archbishop of Toledo. Don Luis's death was a severe blow to Goya, who had become much attached to his patron, who was also a most powerful protector.

When the King expressed his pleasure at Goya's painting for San Francisco el Grande, Goya felt that the coveted appointment of Court Painter was at last

Countess Chinchón,
daughter of the
Infante Don Luis

Maria Teresa de Vallabriga ▶

City on a Rock, one of Goya's fantastic paintings

within his grasp. Indeed, in one of his letters to Zapater he hinted that there were only a few formalities to be completed before his appointment was made official. But he was again doomed to disappointment. King Charles III, who, though he had shown his approval of Goya's work on the tapestry cartoons and on the altarpiece, had from the beginning harboured a violent personal dislike of Goya, refused once more to make him a Court Painter. Francisco had to wait another four years, until the death of the King, before he achieved this, the ambition of every Spanish artist. On the death in 1785 of the Assistant

A new Director of the Academy of San Fernando, Andrea Calleja, Goya was elected
appointment to take his place; this made him one of the most influential figures in the Spanish art world, but it did not compensate him for his failure with the Court. It is

possible that Goya's friendship with Don Luis militated against him, as there was little love lost between the Infante and his brother the King.

One direct result of Goya's success in San Francisco el Grande was a commission to paint that brilliant statesman the Count of Floridablanca himself. The monarchy was gradually slipping into disrepute and it was Floridablanca's self-imposed mission in life to strengthen it, by introducing reforms which, though they seem natural enough today, were revolutionary in the Spain of the period. But with the death of Charles III he found his influence on the Court and the nation supplanted by the Queen's favourite, Godoy. He was also shocked by the events taking place in France. As another of Goya's biographers writes:

'The new ideas in France cooled the heart of Floridablanca. He favoured

The Cardinal Don Luis Maria of
Bourbon and Vallabriga,
son of the Infante Don Luis

55

benevolence towards the people, but not freedom; it upset him to find that there was a growing tendency abroad for them to take as their right what he would not even concede as a possible gift from a kindly sovereign and his ministers.'

The result was that from benevolence Floridablanca flew to the other extreme and instituted repressive measures. No news and, still more, no propaganda of any sort were allowed to filter into Spain. All foreigners, whether resident or visiting, were required to swear allegiance to the King of Spain and to the Roman Catholic religion, and to renounce all claim to protection from their own nations. And, in contradiction to this, he was at the same time appealing for French aid to retain Spanish possession of the whole of the west coast of North America, and war with England was only avoided by the diplomacy of the English Ambassador to Spain. Floridablanca finally fell from office in the autumn of 1792, to be replaced by the Count of Aranda, who, in his turn, was removed to make way for Queen Maria Luisa's favourite, Godoy. In all, Goya painted three portraits of Floridablanca; two of these are in private collections; the third is in the Instituto in Murcia; all three date from the time of the height of his power.

Goya was now in his fortieth year and was entering upon the most brilliant period of his career. As a result of the designs he had already made for the Royal Tapestry Factory, he was in 1786 appointed official painter to the factory. Francisco Bayeu had wanted the appointment for his brother Ramon, but he began to realize that Goya could no longer be suppressed or kept in the background and he put Goya's name forward for it as well. This reconciled the two men, and as a peace-offering Goya painted his brother-in-law. The portrait now hangs in the museum at Valencia.

Reconciliation with Bayeu

There was nothing that Goya liked more than display. He was quite a dandy in his way, always dressed in the height of fashion; and at this period he wore his hair curled and tied at the back with a ribbon. His linen was always impeccable, with ruffles round the neck and at the wrists. He was inordinately vain and was constantly painting self-portraits, of which many have survived. One of his main ambitions was to drive about the streets of Madrid lolling back in his own carriage. The success of his San Francisco painting and the work which it brought him gave him the means of satisfying this ambition; he bought his own carriage, but it was a venture which ended in disaster.

The carriage was a very handsome one, a barouche 'in the English style', of which there were only three in Madrid. Having bought it, he had to try it out, with himself on the box, accompanied by the man who had sold it to him. As he afterwards wrote to Zapater, his progress through the city was a triumphal one, with people in the street stopping to stare at the equipage. As they were proceeding merrily at the gallop, Goya's companion, who was a Neapolitan,

Madrid. The broad prospect of the Calle Alcalá

asked him if he would like to see how the Neapolitans turned. Goya, who was always prepared to learn something new, particularly if it was anything to do with horses, bulls, or sport, said yes he would, and gave the man the reins. Unfortunately, the road was not wide enough for the manœuvre and, instead of turning round, the carriage turned over, landing itself, Francisco, the Neapolitan, and the horse in a ditch. This left Goya temporarily lame in his right leg; of the fate of the other participants in the adventure we know nothing. This cured him of wanting that kind of conveyance, and his next carriage was a sound and solid local one, drawn by steady Aragonese mules.

In spite of Goya's unpopularity at the Court of Charles III, he painted at least two portraits of the King, and they show clearly the antipathy that existed between the two men. The best known of these, the one now in the Prado, was based, in composition, on the portrait of Philip IV in hunting costume by Velazquez. The other one, in Court dress, hangs in the Bank of Spain in Madrid.

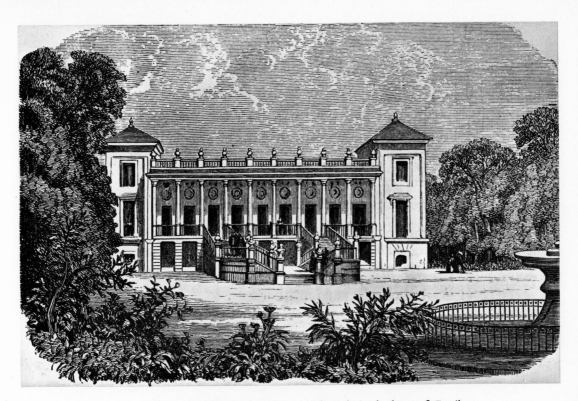

The Duke of Osuna's palace at Alameda in the heart of Castile

It was not long before this, in about 1782, that Goya's connexion with the Osuna family had started. The Ducal family of the Osunas is one of the oldest and the noblest in Spain. In *The Spanish Journal of Lady Holland* we read of the Duchess of Osuna as being 'the most distinguished woman in Madrid for her talents, worth and taste. She has acquired a relish for French luxuries without diminishing her national magnificence and hospitality. She is very lively, and her natural wit covers her total want of refinement and acquirement.' Her only great rival in Madrid society was the Duchess of Alba. Malicious gossip also rumoured that the two duchesses were rivals for the affections of Goya, but the relationship between the painter and the Duchess of Osuna seems never to have progressed beyond one of platonic, if affectionate friendship. It must be noted that, at the time, any society lady who ventured to cross the threshold of Goya's studio was apt to come under suspicion.

Goya's connexion with the Osuna family was one of long duration, and he painted a number of portraits of its members and executed an even larger

The Osuna family

The Picnic. One of Goya's many charming studies of the everyday life of the time

number of commissions from the Duke and Duchess for paintings on a variety of subjects; the Osuna Collection was sold in 1896 and is now distributed all over Europe, many of the pictures being now either in the Prado or in the Academy of San Fernando in Madrid. The most important of the Osuna portraits is *The Duke of Osuna and his Family*, painted in about 1785 and now in the Prado. Two of the Osuna collection are in the National Gallery, London—*El Hechizado por Fuerza* ('The Bewitched by Force') and *La Merienda* ('The Picnic'). One of the most remarkable pictures in the collection is *La*

The Duke of Osuna and his Family ▶

The Pilgrimage of San Isidro, a panoramic view of the popular feast in honour of St Isidore

Romería de San Isidro ('The Pilgrimage of San Isidro'), now in the Prado; although it measures only about three feet by one foot, it contains a mass of detail and figures in the foreground, with Madrid on the skyline in the background, and is amazing in its broadness and depth.

Prices received by artists for their work are always matters of interest to later generations, and records of the prices paid by the Osunas have been preserved. They varied, when translated into English money, between £26 and £41. Even taking into consideration the vastly greater purchasing power of money in those days, and particularly in Spain, these prices do not seem to be exorbitant; Goya was, however, a diligent and a quick worker, and from all accounts seems to have lived very comfortably on the proceeds of his work.

An early print of the Convent of San Isidro

The portraits of the Osuna family are not among Goya's best work. It is often said about him that he did not really begin to find himself as a portrait painter until the beginning of the nineteenth century; but such a portrait as that of Maria Ana Monino, Marquesa de Pontejos, the Count of Floridablanca's sister-in-law, painted in the late 1780's, and now in the National Gallery, Washington, seems to belie this contention. This is one of his best-known and finest pictures, and Hugh Stokes's description brings it vividly before our eyes:

'One may search the galleries of Europe to find a more perfect specimen of rococo art. The Marquesa de Pontejos is the personification of the *grande dame* who endeavoured to be in the fashion when Rousseau preached a return to nature and Marie Antoinette played at rusticity in the gardens of the Trianon.

The young Marquesa, tightly laced, fluttering with furbelows, frills and ribbons, a mass of vapid but engaging extravagance, chaperoned by a tiny pug which shakes the silver bells jingling from his collar, stares from the artist's canvas with a gaze half insolence, half challenge. Her eyes are beautiful, but they reveal the littleness of her soul and the poverty of her mind. In her right hand she nonchalantly holds a flower, and she slowly advances as if to dance—not a fandango, but a formal minuet in the manner of Versailles. The Marquesa de Pontejos represents the influence of French fashion over the wealthier circles of Spanish Society.'

Charles IV

When, in December 1788, Charles III died, Court prejudice against Goya died with him. The new King, Charles IV, had always been well disposed towards the painter and on his ascent to the throne took him under his patronage. The King was forty years of age at the time, just two years younger than his protégé. He was a man of weak character and of limited intelligence, whose only real interest in life was hunting. Some years after his abdication in 1807 he admitted to Napoleon: 'While I was king I rose each morning, heard Mass, had breakfast and hunted until one o'clock. After dinner I hunted again while the light lasted. In the evening Manuel Godoy came and made his daily report to me on affairs of State. Then I went to bed, to repeat the same routine next day.' The Court was, in fact, dominated by the Queen, Maria Luisa, who, in turn, was dominated by her favourite, Manuel de Godoy. Godoy was born in Badajoz, in southern Spain, in 1767, which makes him only twenty-one at the time Charles IV succeeded to the Spanish throne. He came from a very old, noble but impoverished family. He was endowed with a fine physique, good looks, geniality, ambition, and a certain cunning, and of these attributes he made the very best possible use. At the age of seventeen he obtained a commission in the Guardias de la Real Persona—the King's personal bodyguard—and as such was in constant attendance on the Royal Family and the Court. With the advantages that he possessed, it was not surprising that he soon attracted the attention of Princess Maria Luisa of Parma, wife of the Prince of the Asturias, the heir to the throne; her amours were already common gossip, but her attach-

Godoy

ment to the young Godoy was to be the most permanent of them all. Everyone in Spain, or at any rate in Madrid, was aware of the state of affairs except, as so often, the deceived husband. Even the reigning King was aware of it. There is a tale that the Prince of the Asturias once remarked to his father how difficult it was for women of the Royal Family to commit adultery because 'there were so few people of equal rank and they have so few opportunities'. Charles IV merely replied: 'What a fool you are, Carlos! What a blind fool!'

On the death of Charles III, Godoy's rise was rapid, but so was his eclipse. By 1792 he was Premier; banished in 1798, he returned to office in 1801 and

65

Charles IV, *King of Spain*

clung on until 1808 when an outbreak at Aranjuez drove him into hiding. He was captured and imprisoned until Napoleon secured his release, and he rejoined Charles IV and Maria Luisa in exile in Bayonne. When Charles died he returned to Madrid for a short time, in an endeavour to recover some of his property that had been confiscated. In this he failed and the rest of his life was passed in poverty and obscurity; he died in Paris in 1851, at the age of eighty-four. He wrote his *Mémoires*, which were published in Spanish, French, and English and which form valuable *matériel pour servir* in the history of the period. He was an admirer and a friend of Goya's, a fact which may be partly accounted for by a fellow-feeling, in that both men had been thwarted by Charles III.

Maria Luisa, Queen of Spain ▶

Manuel Godoy, 'Prince of the Peace' and royal favourite

Appointed Court Painter

Charles IV, like his father, made a pretence of being interested in the arts. In this he was encouraged by Godoy, who persuaded the King to appoint Goya to the position of Court Painter, thus realizing Francisco's ambition of many years, which the late King had never satisfied. And from that time forward Goya painted numerous portraits of the Royal Family. It is difficult to decide which is the best of these, though an outstanding picture is the portrait of Maria Luisa in the Prado, painted in 1790, when the Queen was about forty, although she looked some fifteen years older. The companion portrait of the King, painted at the same time, is not so impressive.

There are only two recorded portraits of Godoy by Goya. One, entitled *Don Manuel Godoy, Duke of Alcudia, Prince of the Peace*, hangs in the Prado, while the other, an equestrian portrait, has disappeared. This is all the more strange considering how much time Goya spent during the last decade of the century at the various royal palaces, painting members of the Royal Family

The Parasol ▶

A view of Valencia from the entrance of the Alameida

and the Court. There are at least ten portraits of Charles IV in existence and more still of the Queen; in spite of her ugliness, or perhaps because of it, painting her seemed to have a peculiar fascination for him; the portraits are distributed all over the world; one of the most brilliant of them is hung, oddly enough, in the Museo de Arte Moderno in Madrid, where it stands out, at the end of a long gallery, like a torch shining in a darkened room.

It was at about this time that Goya's health began to suffer. He suddenly seemed to be obsessed by the spectre of death, little realizing that he was to live for nearly another forty years. He was also worried about his wife's health, and that of his children. Josefa having been ordered to the seaside, her husband accompanied her on a visit to Valencia, where he spent most of his time hunting; but found time to paint two large pictures which he presented to the Academía de San Carlos there in October 1790, being elected a member of that institution by the grateful recipients.

The Duchess of Alba,
the most celebrated beauty
of her day in Spain

*The Duchess of
Alba*

We now come to the vexed story of Goya and the Duchess of Alba, about which there has been so much speculation during the past hundred and eighty years. They probably first met in 1789, possibly through the Duchess of Osuna, when the Duchess of Alba was twenty-seven or twenty-eight and Goya forty-three. Dona Maria Teresa Cayetana de Silva y Alvarez de Toledo, to give her only a few of her styles and titles, was thirteenth Duchess of Alba in her own right, having succeeded her grandfather in 1776, at the age of fourteen, when she was already married to the eleventh Marquis of Villafranca, an obscure but extremely rich nobleman, about whom little is known except that he loved music. In accordance with Spanish custom in such cases, the husband took his wife's title and became the Duke of Alba. At the time when she met Goya, Maria Teresa shared with the Duchess of Osuna the undisputed leadership of Madrid society. This infuriated Queen Maria Luisa, who, in spite of her superior rank, could not hope to compete with the duchesses either in beauty or in wit. Besides, the Queen was a foreigner, which made her unpopular with the haughty Spanish nobility. Many stories are told of attempts on the part of Maria Luisa to humiliate the Duchess of Alba, and of the Duchess's retaliations. One authenticated tale is that when the Queen ordered herself some new dresses from Paris, the Duchess dressed her maids in copies of them and made them parade in open carriages in the Paseo del Prado, to the amusement of the populace. There was also considerable friction between the two duchesses over their romantic affairs.

Goya painted the Duchess of Alba at least a dozen times, though only nine of the portraits have her name definitely ascribed to them. One of the best of these is that which hangs in the Liria Palace in Madrid. It is a fulllength portrait in a rather haughty pose; Maria Teresa is wearing a white dress of shimmering silk. Her waist is gathered in with a wide red silk sash, one end

The Young Duke of Alba

The Duchess of Alba
(detail from the painting)

of which hangs down; a red bow adorns her breast and another is placed in the magnificent black hair that cascades down to her waist. A necklace of red beads, probably coral, is round her neck. At her feet stands a small white dog, and this too seems to have a red bow on its tail. By way of jewellery the Duchess wears only two wide gold bangles on her left arm and wrist. It is not, perhaps, one of Goya's best portraits, but this may be accounted for by his obsession with the personality of the subject, which distracted his mind and his brush. The forefinger of her right hand is pointed to an inscription painted on the ground: 'A la duquesa de Alba. Fco. de Goya. 1795.'

Two years later, in 1797, he painted his most famous portrait of the Duchess in a black mantilla. In it she seems more masterful than ever, with an air of imperious calmness. She wears a bright yellow bodice with long sleeves and cuffs of gold lace; a crimson silk sash—red was always her favourite colour—encircles her waist. As in the 1795 portrait, her finger points to an inscription on the ground, bearing Goya's name and the date 1797. On the pointing hand she wears two rings: the one on the third finger is marked 'Alba'; the one on the extended finger bears the name 'Goya'. Do we need further proof of their romance? The picture now hangs in the Metropolitan Museum of Art in New York.

One important painting of this period is really little more than a sketch and shows the artist himself greeting the Duchess. It was painted a little earlier than the other two, and has something of the caricature about it. Goya represents himself as a man of fashion in a long-tailed coat, tight breeches, a high collar, and high boots. The Duchess, in black with a black mantilla, smiles as she points to the gathering storm-clouds, while in her left hand she holds a half-opened fan.

This picture, which is now in the collection of the Marqués de Romana in Madrid, was painted in 1793, the year when Queen Maria Luisa wreaked her vengeance on the Duchess by banishing her to her estates in Andalusia. Goya immediately applied to the King for leave of absence from his duties as Court Painter, and accompanied her to Sanlúcar. There he remained, refusing to leave the Duchess until, in the following year, she was released from exile, this being, it appears, the only way by which Goya could be persuaded to return to Madrid. During the journey to Sanlúcar, at a lonely place named Despena Perros, they had an accident, in which the back axle of the coach was damaged. Goya, with characteristic energy, lit a fire in which to heat the axle so that he could bend it straight again. Becoming overheated himself, he caught a chill, which finally resulted in complete deafness, an infirmity which overshadowed the remainder of his life.

The Duchess's dwelling near Sanlúcar was a large country house named the Palacio del Rocío, after a hermitage in the vicinity. It no longer exists today, nor is there any painting or engraving or even a description of it.

The Duke of Alba died in Seville in 1796, and Maria Teresa retired for a short period of widowhood to her Sanlúcar estates, where she was again joined by Goya. But the romance was waning, and by the middle of the following year the Duchess, perhaps belatedly recalled to the dignity due to her rank, and also tiring of her lover's deafness, seems to have passed out of his life. Little more is heard of her until her death in 1802, at the age of forty. On her death her property was seized and sold by the Crown. Among her pictures was the so-called Rokeby Venus, which passed into Godoy's hands and is now in the National Gallery, London.

The Duchess of Alba was the deepest and most real passion in Goya's life, which was otherwise taken up by his art. She was a vain and a not very intelligent woman, ill-educated, as were nearly all Spanish women of the period, but possessing great beauty and a pride of race that made an irresistible appeal to a man of Goya's comparatively humble origin. She has come down to us as one of the world's *femmes fatales* and yet, had it not been for Goya's portraits of her, her name would have been forgotten today: such is the power of great artists to immortalize their subjects, and such their responsibility to posterity. The

Goya and the Duchess of Alba

romance influenced Goya's art to the end of his life. Maria Teresa's features are constantly reappearing in his later paintings, and not always in very kind contexts. The bitterness that he felt at his abandonment is best illustrated by *Los Caprichos*, those cynical comments on the life and morals of his times. In these her face recurs, as in *El Sueño de la Mentira y de la Inconstancia* ('The Dream of Lies and Inconstancy'), where she appears as a two-faced woman with one arm clutched by Goya himself and her other hand held by a two-faced man and an evil-looking, witch-like woman.

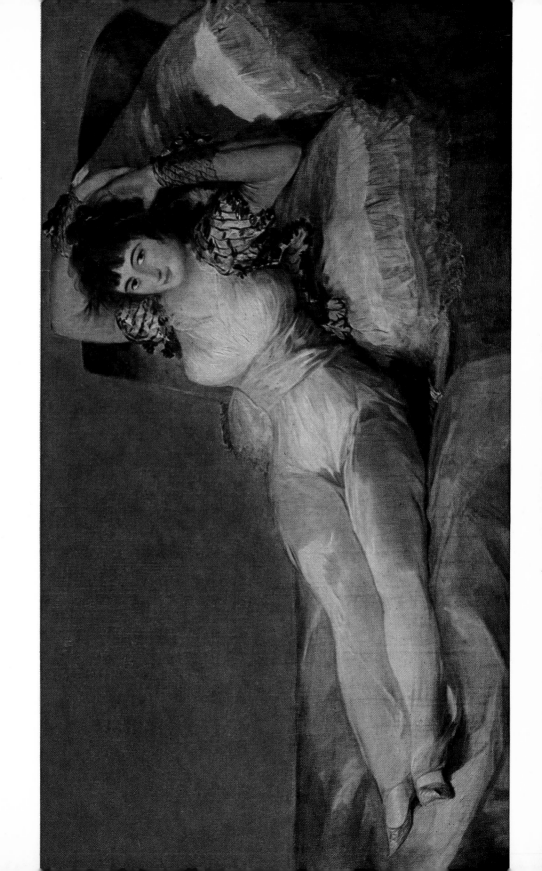

A Maja with two bull-fighters

The Duchess of Alba cannot be dismissed from the story of Goya's life without reference being made to his two famous pictures, *La Maja Desnuda* and *La Maja Vestida*—'The Naked Maja' and 'The Clothed Maja'—which have always been associated with Maria Teresa's name.

In considering these pictures we are confronted, at the outset, with the task of defining the status of the *Maja* in the Spanish life of the period. The *Maja* was the feminine companion of the *Majo*, a man of the people, an aristocrat of the underworld, a gallant who dressed in flamboyant clothes, a hero to the populace,

Lady with a little negro child—a sketch by Goya

an idler who, like the lilies of the field, toiled not, neither did he spin. He lived on his wits or, if they were not sharp enough to support him, on one or more of his *Majas*. Perhaps his nearest equivalent in modern times would be the Paris *apache*. Goya was always fascinated by these people and produced many paintings and etchings in which they figured; but of all of them the two mentioned above are the best known.

The Naked Maja The story usually told about them is that Goya persuaded the Duchess of Alba to pose as the 'Naked Maja', and that the Duke got wind of this and determined to confront Goya with what he considered to be an unpardonable affront to himself. Goya, however, was warned and swiftly painted *The Clothed Maja* to show His Grace when he arrived at his studio. But there are several reasons why we should treat this story with reserve.

In the first place, it is very unlikely that Goya, swift worker though he was, would have had time to paint such a finished picture as *The Clothed Maja*. Secondly, had he aimed at appeasing the Duke's wrath, he would hardly have tried to do so with *The Clothed Maja*, which is really the more voluptuous of

the two. And, most relevant of all, the pictures bear no resemblance to the Duchess, either in face or in figure. Finally, the Prado authorities—whose opinion is at least as good as, and probably better than, anyone else's—comment in their catalogue: 'It is indisputable that the Duchess of Alba did not sit for either of these two pictures.' Pedro de Madrazo, who wrote this, declared that the model was a girl who was the mistress of one of Goya's friends. The two pictures originally belonged to the Duchess and hung in the Liria Palace in Madrid—another good reason why they should not have been of her. On her death they passed into Godoy's hands. They were next heard of in the Academy of San Fernando and are now in the Prado, where they occupy a prominent position.

In 1795 Goya resigned from his appointment to the Royal Tapestry Factory of Santa Bárbara. The reason given was that his health was deteriorating, but it is more likely that he felt tied down by his appointment there and was also getting more portrait commissions than he could conveniently cope with. In the same year his brother-in-law Francisco Bayeu died, and in October the Academy of

The report on Goya's
petition to become
First Court Painter

San Fernando elected Goya to succeed him as Director of the School of
Painting. His deafness, however, proved an insuperable obstacle, and eighteen
months later he resigned with the title of 'Honorary Director'. And in homage
to his brother-in-law he painted a posthumous portrait of Bayeu, copying, with
certain minor alterations, a self-portrait of him. This picture is now to be seen
in the Prado; the only other portrait that Goya painted of Bayeu is the one,
already referred to, which is now in the museum at Valencia.

Goya returned to Madrid from Sanlúcar by a circuitous route, taking in
Cadiz and Saragossa on the way. While in Cadiz he painted a picture of the
Last Supper for the Church of Santa Cueva; in this he disregarded the tradi-
tional grouping of the Apostles as typified by Leonardo da Vinci's famous
treatment of the same subject, and showed them cowering on the floor in terror
as they grasped the fact that their Master had been betrayed. It was such a
complete departure from convention that anyone but Goya would have had his
painting rejected.

Los Caprichos: They already have a seat   *Los Caprichos: To his grandfather*

His visit to Saragossa was probably a reaction from the atmosphere of Sanlúcar; he sought to rid himself of its memory by returning to the scene of his childhood, and also perhaps hoped to renew acquaintanceship with old friends, particularly Martin Zapater. Alas! his friendship with Zapater, which dated from boyhood's days, was gradually dying out; the two old friends had little left in common. Their lives had drifted too far apart; besides which, Zapater disapproved of Goya's way of life, especially his desertion of Josefa for long periods while he was dallying with the Duchess of Alba and other ladies of the Court. Their correspondence, which had been constant and voluminous in the early years, became more and more desultory and ceased altogether at about the end of the century. But, during this visit to Saragossa, Goya painted a portrait of his old friend, having previously painted him in 1790.

It was during that last visit of his to Sanlúcar that Goya laid the foundation for the series of etchings to which he subsequently gave the name of *Los Caprichos*. Like other artists, he was in the habit of carrying about notebooks in which to

Los Caprichos

Los Caprichos: Correction

make rough sketches for future drawings and paintings as they occurred to him. He must have seen that his great romance was coming to an end, and he was becoming disgusted with the world of intrigue and make-believe and deceit in which he found himself involved; and, above all, he was beginning to be disillusioned with the Duchess of Alba. The physical attraction was still there and would remain with him until long after her death, but he now realized that Maria Teresa's life was ruled by her whims and caprices.

Many other artists and critics have declared that they consider *Los Caprichos* to be Goya's finest work. They are possibly his most original work, but they cannot compare in craftsmanship with the best of his portraits. One of his early biographers described them as 'a picaresque novel'. Their central theme is that everything is a lie and that all women are deceivers; and through them all the features of the Duchess of Alba constantly recur. Other subsidiary themes run through *Los Caprichos*: the perils that beset young and innocent girls, witchcraft (a subject that always interested Goya, and for which brutal punishment was still being meted out in Spain at the end of the eighteenth century), the abuses of the clergy in general, and of the Inquisition in particular.

A meeting of the Spanish Inquisition

Los Caprichos were announced for publication in a series of seventy-two in 1797, but this was delayed until February 1799, when a series of eighty plates was put on sale in Madrid. The etchings had been on sale for only a few days before they were withdrawn, owing to the indignation they caused among Society ladies and the clergy, who recognized themselves or at least their counterparts in these harsh portrayals. In fact, Goya was in grave danger of being arraigned before the Inquisition, and only the unexpected intervention of the King himself saved him from the attentions of the Holy Office. Goya had dedicated the etchings to the King, and he now offered him the original plates. King Charles IV was a very stupid man and it is improbable that he had the remotest idea of the implications of *Los Caprichos*, but he was also a very vain man, who liked to be considered a patron of the arts, so he accepted them, thus relieving Goya of any further awkwardness. In those days royalty, particularly Spanish royalty, never accepted gifts without granting something in return. Goya asked nothing for himself but obtained for his son Xavier, on whom he doted and of whom he once said that he was 'the most beautiful child in Madrid', an annuity of 12,000 reales—only £150 in English

The Church of
San Antonio de la Florida

money, but quite a considerable sum for a middle-class man in those days in Spain.

Frescoes for
San Antonio de
la Florida

In 1792 the Church of San Antonio de la Florida, originally part of the hermitage of the same name on the northern outskirts of Madrid, was reconstructed. It stood in a property belonging to the King, who commissioned Goya to undertake its decoration. The frescoes, which he began in June 1798, remain to this day one of the principal monuments to his art. Goya always said that his three masters were Velazquez, Rembrandt, and Nature, and in his work in San Antonio he showed himself to be an apt pupil of these masters.

Many attempts have been made to describe these frescoes, but they are so divided up by the various corners and convolutions of the church that it is only by looking at them that they can be really appreciated; and even then the church is so dimly lit that it is difficult to see them properly. Their main charm is their complete lack of conventionality. Goya was no longer hampered in his work by his brother-in-law or by committees of priests and city dignitaries, as he had been in most of his other church decorations, particularly in Saragossa.

The cupola of San Antonio de la Florida, with Goya's frescoes

He was directly responsible only to the King, who, knowing nothing about art himself, put his entire trust in Goya, who was thus able to give his imagination full rein.

The cupola of the church bears a picture of Saint Anthony of Padua raising a murdered man from the dead so that he might reveal the identity of his assassin: in itself rather a macabre theme, but one which is relieved by the rest of the decorations which support it. Around the base of the cupola there are more than a hundred over-life-size figures, among whom can be recognized many of the fashionable men and women of the period. They are all enclosed by a balcony, or seated behind it, some in earnest conversation with one another, some contemplating the miracle being performed by Saint Anthony, and some merely gazing down into the interior of the church. Angels adorn the corners and niches. Nothing that Goya ever painted has received such extremes of favourable and unfavourable criticism, which persist to this day.

A detail from
the cupola of
San Antonio
de la Florida

Goya has often been accused of being a revolutionary and a republican; but this is not true. He was a man of quick temper and an individualist who refused to be bound down by either tradition or convention when they did not suit his mood or his inspiration. This, together with the anti-clericalism which he showed in many of his works, particularly in *Los Caprichos*, made him an object of suspicion at a time when the country was seething with unrest, and anyone who departed from the rigid lines of conduct expected of the individual was likely to attract the attention of the still all-powerful Inquisition. The fact is that Goya was an ardent patriot who ridiculed the many abuses of power and privilege which he saw around him; anyone who did that was bound to incur the displeasure of the personages of whom he disapproved and they, in order to justify themselves, attacked him and accused him of having subversive ideas.

Goya's self-portrait,
painted *c.* 1800

As a result of Goya's work in San Antonio de la Florida, which he com-pleted in a remarkably short space of time, he was appointed First Painter to the King, the highest honour bestowed upon any Spanish painter of the period.

Becomes First
Court Painter

This is a biography of Goya, not a history of Spain. But we must not forget the background of the times in which he lived, which had such a marked effect upon his painting. Though his deafness was apt to isolate him from everyday life, he must have been aware of the fact that Spain declared war on England in 1795, and that Godoy, one of his staunchest patrons, fell from grace in 1798. All the same, he carried on with his portraits, particularly in Court circles, and it is to this period (1799–1800) that we owe one of the best of his royal pictures, the group of King Charles IV and Queen Maria Luisa with their entire family (see colour plate facing page 116).

The Infanta Maria Josefa

The picture was painted at the Royal Palace of Aranjuez, where Goya devoted a considerable amount of time and thought to it. He made careful studies of each of the figures; most of these studies have been preserved, many of them being in the Prado. There are thirteen members of the family in the finished picture; they are all standing, the central figures being the King and Queen and the Queen's youngest son, Francisco de Paula, whose paternity is usually ascribed to Godoy. The fact that the family consisted of thirteen people presented a difficulty, as the Spanish are deeply superstitious, and the number thirteen is considered even more unlucky in Spain than elsewhere. But Goya, who often introduced his own portrait into his paintings, used the device to solve this difficulty—he appears in the background, in front of an easel. In this instance it might have been more appropriate if he had inserted a portrait of Manuel de Godoy in the background.

This is the most successful group that Goya ever painted. He was not at his best with groups; his pictures of the Osuna and Montijo families show them clearly for what they are, namely a number of portraits painted separately and then pieced together like a jigsaw puzzle.

During the next twenty years Goya painted some of his finest, but not all his best-known portraits. Hitherto, although his life was dominated by his art, there were also the urgent calls of his strong and passionate nature and his thirst for adventure. But as he grew older and the fires of youth died down, he became more and more absorbed in his art to the exclusion of everything else. So the story of his later life is mostly the story of his paintings. He possessed to a remarkable degree that quality which is so often lacking in artists, of being able to sink his own personality in that of his subjects.

Goya's great portraits

The Infante Don Francisco de Paula Antonio

To this period belong the equestrian portrait of General Don José Palafox, Duke of Saragossa, in the Prado. There is also the portrait of the French Ambassador to Spain, Ferdinand Guillemardet, done in 1798 and now in the Louvre. In it Goya revelled in the colours of the tricolor and gold sash and the hat with its red, white, and blue ostrich feathers which formed the official uniform of all the more important functionaries of the Republic; the Ambassador himself seems to be almost of secondary importance, and yet as a portrait this painting is superb.

Yet another notable portrait of this period shows Godoy in the uniform of a captain-general, reclining against a rock behind a scene of battle and studying a map at arm's length. An aide-de-camp is in attendance in the background, and a Portuguese standard at the left of the picture commemorates the preposterous expedition which Godoy led in person against Portugal in the French interests in 1801. This 'invasion' met with no resistance, but Godoy claimed it as a major victory and sent the Queen an orange-branch as a token; whence it was called the 'War of the Oranges'. This dates Goya's picture, which now hangs in the Academy of San Fernando, at the end of 1801.

The Studio of Goya, an imaginary reconstruction

Portrait of Ferdinand Guillemardet, the French Ambassador ▶

The actress,
Doña Antonia Zarate

There is nothing of Goya's that can be certainly assigned to the following year, though there is no reason to suppose that he was idle. *Los Caprichos* were reissued in 1803, with a self-portrait etched by Goya as its frontispiece. And in about 1805 he painted one of the best of his portraits of women, that of Doña Antonia Zarate. One feels that there was deep sympathy between artist and sitter. She was a sick woman, dying of consumption, and she possessed the pale ethereal beauty which so often accompanies that condition; her large dark eyes and slightly smiling lips show a proud resignation to her fate.

From this period also dates the portrait of Goya's son Xavier as a young man. He is dressed as a man of fashion, almost a dandy; his features closely resemble those of his father, but lack their forcefulness. In it can be seen the great pride Goya had for this his favourite son and the only one of his twenty children to survive him, and the joy that he felt in having been able to lift him out of the working-class surroundings in which he himself had been brought up.

Goya's portrait of his son, Xavier ▶

93

Ferdinand VII, King of Spain

The last decade of the eighteenth century saw the whole of Europe in a ferment. Spain's attempt at a campaign against France in 1793 had ended in miserable failure and capitulation, and by the Treaty of San Idelfonso in 1796 Spain agreed to assist France against the English, declaring war on Great Britain two months later. This also was a disastrous war for Spain, lasting six years and costing her Trinidad. In the meantime she came more and more under the domination of France. In 1807 Napoleon sent a force of 30,000 men under General Junot to Lisbon with the object of conquering Portugal and dividing it up between France and Spain; and in 1808, under the pretext of reinforcing Junot's army, he sent a further 100,000 troops under Murat across the Pyrenees with the permission of the Spanish Government; that is to say, of Godoy. As the French troops advanced, hatred of the foreigner reached boiling-point in Madrid, and only the abdication of Charles IV in favour of his son, who became Ferdinand VII, saved Godoy's neck. The ex-King and Queen fled to Bayonne, where they were later joined by Godoy.

Napoleon invades Spain

The Disasters of War, An unhappy mother

All these upheavals distressed Goya, who, cut off from the world as he was by his deafness, could not fully grasp the meaning of it all. However, he accepted the new monarch philosophically and one of his first duties was to paint him, though the portrait was not finished when Ferdinand, in his turn, went into exile and Napoleon put his elder brother, Joseph Bonaparte, on the Spanish throne.

These events were the background to his pictures of episodes during the French invasion of 1808, and also *Los Desastres de la Guerra* ('The Disasters of War') the series of eighty etchings which he made during or shortly after the French occupation. Everything points to the fact that the martyrdom of Spain under the French made a deep impression on Goya. He may have exaggerated the atrocities—but in due fairness to the French it should be remembered that the war was a very violent one, and that in the bitterness of their humiliation the Spanish guerrillas did not show much mercy to the French occupiers once they fell into their hands.

The Second of May

In May 1808, Napoleon's General Murat and 25,000 French soldiers entered Madrid. The population was seething with patriotic fury and massed, practi‑cally unarmed, in the Puerta del Sol, the hub and centre of the city. They could have been dealt with quite easily and without bloodshed, but Murat, angered by Spanish resistance to what was, after all, a *fait accompli*, set his troops on to the mob and butchered them.

Goya was in Madrid at the time of this massacre. He may even have witnessed it; he was certainly in the vicinity and saw the aftermath. And this inspired two of the most famous of his pictures, entitled *The Second of May* and *The Third of May* respectively; both now hang in the Prado, where they attract the attention of thousands of visitors by their sheer realism and brutality. The first shows the

The Third of May

combat, if it can be called a combat, between the *madrileños* and the
Mamelukes of the French Imperial Guard in the Puerta del Sol. The second
shows the mass execution, on the following day, of anyone caught in Madrid
bearing any form of offensive weapon or even being suspected of being anti-
French, a description which must have embraced almost the entire population
of the city. The figures in both these pictures are life-size; the actual date of their
painting is in dispute. Goya certainly made sketches for them at the time, but
probably did not paint them until later. Other pictures of his, dealing with
incidents of the occupation and of the Spanish resistance, are also to be found
in the Prado, and there is a picture in the Royal Palace of Madrid showing
Spanish patriots manufacturing munitions in the mountains outside the capital.

Goya's last self-portrait

An episode during the War of Independence: guerrillas making bullets in the forest

Notwithstanding all this, when Joseph Bonaparte was shortly afterwards installed in Madrid as King of Spain, Goya accepted the confirmation of his office as First Court Painter. He has been blamed for this and accused of treason, but, with a great many other of his more thoughtful compatriots, he realized that the sorry state into which Spain had drifted was almost entirely due to the disastrous policy, or rather the lack of any kind of policy, of Godoy and Maria Luisa, while the King was no more than a figurehead in the administration. Spain had reached almost her lowest ebb, and if anything could lift her out of the mire it was a completely new government and entirely new blood; even foreign blood. Those men who had the welfare of Spain really at heart realized this and decided to give the new administration a chance.

Despite the presence of *el rey intruso*—'the Intruder King'—there was no longer any pretence of friendship between France and Spain. Spain and Portugal rose against the French and appealed for help to England. On August 3, 1808, the first British troops landed in Mondego Bay in Portugal. Thus began the Peninsular War which was to devastate Spain and Portugal for the next six years.

The Spanish War

During these years information about Goya is scanty. He was caught up in the second siege of Saragossa, nobly but unsuccessfully defended by his old friend Palafox, at the turn of the year 1808. In February 1810 he was commissioned by the Municipal Council in Madrid to paint Joseph Bonaparte; but the King proved to be elusive, while the only portrait of him that Goya was able to get hold of was a print originating in Rome and showing him in profile. Whether he ever executed the portrait or not remains something of a mystery; whenever a reference to it is made it is said either to be 'in private hands' or to have been lost. But Goya did paint an allegorical picture entitled *The City of Madrid*, the central figure of which is a beautiful young woman representing the capital. On the left of the picture is a shield bearing the arms of the city; there are other figures, whose purpose is not very clear, including two winged spirits, one of them blowing a trumpet. Also a dog; Goya was very fond of introducing dogs into his pictures. On the right of the picture is a large medallion which originally contained a portrait of Joseph Bonaparte in profile, taken from the Italian print. This medallion passed through a series of vicissitudes. When King Joseph was deposed, his portrait was painted out and the word 'Constitución' substituted. This was later replaced by a portrait of Ferdinand VII, which in turn suffered eclipse when a reproduction of the Book of the Constitution was substituted. And finally this too was removed, the words 'Dos de Mayo' (May 2) being put in its place, in memory of the slaughter in the Puerta del Sol; and it is in this condition that it can now be seen in the Town Hall of Madrid.

During the next two or three years Goya painted several members of Joseph's entourage, including General Guye and his nephew Victor Guye, General Joseph Quérault, and a man who really was a traitor to Spain, José Manuel Romero, Minister of the Interior and of Police, who had thrown in his lot with the Intruder King. But Goya painted these portraits in an almost mechanical way, without any interest in his sitters.

In October 1810 three Spanish painters were asked to select fifty beautiful Spanish pictures for the 'Napoleon Museum' in Paris. The painters charged with this task were Goya, Maella, and Napoli. The task put these three painters in a difficult position. If they refused to undertake it, another committee would be appointed who might take the commission seriously. If they consented they would be accused of being *afrancesado*, i.e. frenchified, or, in modern parlance, collaborators: also, they would have to include some at least of Spain's art treasures, so as to avoid suspicion. They finally agreed and selected three paintings by Velazquez, two by Murillo, four by Ribera, and five by Zurbaran, none of them, of course, being among the finer work of these masters; all the others were pictures of comparatively little importance, though there was a sufficient

Goya's *Allegory of the City of Madrid* ▶

A woman attacked by brigands

nucleus of great names to satisfy the authorities. The selectors showed an appropriate sense of humour by choosing, as one of the paintings by Velazquez, *Joseph's Bloodstained Coat*, presumably with Joseph Bonaparte in mind. In point of fact, the pictures were never sent to France; some were stolen, some destroyed, and the rest returned to the places whence they came. As a result of his activities at this time, Goya was awarded the Order of Spain, instituted by King Joseph and bestowed on people whom he considered to be helpful to him in his rule; this order was contemptuously known as the 'Egg-plant' and was abolished with the expulsion of Joseph. Goya himself never wore it, which was just as well for him, as, with the restoration of Ferdinand VII, the people who had worn it were accused of high treason.

Following on the landing of British troops on the Peninsula, the whole of Spain was thrown into an even worse state of disorder. Banditry had been

El Empecinado,
one of the most redoubtable
Spanish guerrilla leaders

rife for years, but now the robber bands organized themselves into guerrilla forces to harry and terrorize the invader. One of the most feared and intrepid of these marauders was Juan Martín, the son of a cobbler, who was known, not without reason, as El Empecinado—the Indomitable. He made such a nuisance of himself that Joseph sent General Hugo, Governor of Guadalajara, and, incidentally, Victor Hugo's father, to disperse his band and take him prisoner. El Empecinado evaded capture, but the General was so impressed by his fine qualities as a leader that he wrote to him urging him to change his allegiance and come to fight by his side for the liberty of Spain. Goya painted El Empecinado later, after the Restoration; it is one of his finest portraits of the later period and on looking at it one understands why its subject was given his name. He also painted a number of important pictures of the lives and activities of the robber bands.

The Disasters of War: See who is strong

The troubles that beset Goya at this time had their effect on him, and his health, which had shown some improvement, began once more to worry him. For a time he gave up the more arduous work of portrait-painting to return to etching, and it was then that he produced *Los Desastres de la Guerra*. These follow logically on *Los Caprichos*, in that they lay bare the horrors of a great social evil. They are an appalling indictment of war, without any attempt at minimizing its miseries, and depict the atrocities attributed to the French invaders. Interspersed with them are pictures showing the plight of the monks and nuns who wandered over the countryside without any means whatever of support, and often resorted to plundering with the bandits. On the orders of Napoleon, two-thirds of the monasteries and convents in Spain had been suppressed, their buildings destroyed, and their occupants driven into the open to fend for themselves as best they might; as most of them had hitherto lived cloistered lives, they had no means whatever of earning an honest living.

▲ *This also*: monks fleeing from the French invaders   *I saw this as well*, Goya's view of the inhumanity of war ▼

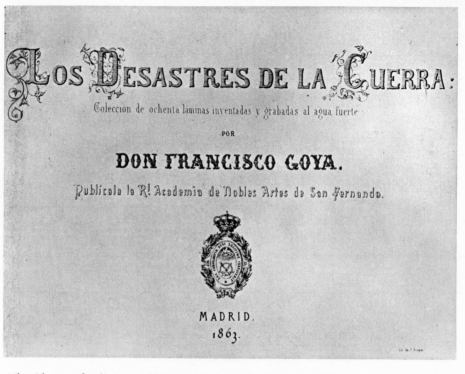

The title-page for the first published edition of *The Disasters of War*

The Disasters of War were probably not intended for general circulation but were a form of self-expression by which Goya needed to get out of his system the horrors and miseries with which he was surrounded. They were produced between the years 1810 and 1813, but apart from a few artist's proofs which Goya would naturally need in order to see how his finished work would appear, they were not publicly issued in his lifetime. Indeed, they were first issued in a limited edition thirty-five years after his death, in 1863, by the Academy of San Fernando. They have frequently been reissued from the original plates until these are almost worn out; the 1863 issue consists of the first and therefore the most brilliant pulls; it was limited to a small number and is very rare.

Goya shows a true picture of war in his *Disasters*. Not for him the soldiers strutting through the streets to the sound of martial music, acclaimed and garlanded by hysterical crowds for whom all that matters is the glorious aftermath. He is concerned with the truth of war, its dirt, disease, squalor, cruelty, and slime; and he has depicted it in a manner that no other artist has ever succeeded in doing. The lesson is, 'There is no heroism in war.'

Goya's sketch of
'The Iron Duke'

Seven months after the first British troops landed in Portugal, the Duke of Wellington, then Sir Arthur Wellesley, arrived in Lisbon to take over their command. The Peninsular War was running its course. On August 10, 1812, after the Battle of Salamanca, Joseph Bonaparte fled from Madrid, and two days later Wellington, now in supreme command of all the British, Spanish, and Portuguese troops, entered the capital in triumph, with General Alava by his side. At the head of the Spanish irregulars rode El Empecinado, while the people lined the streets, hysterical with joy at their liberation, and shouted 'Viva Velinton!'

Goya and Wellington

It is not surprising that Goya, as a Spanish patriot in spite of his enforced connexion with Joseph, should immediately make friends with the new arrivals, and one of his first moves was to get permission to paint Wellington. The Iron Duke had a strong prejudice against artists of all kinds, particularly painters, and there are many stories told of his subterfuges to avoid having his portrait painted; he was convinced that there was so little sympathy between the soldier and the artist that no painter could possibly do a soldier justice. He thought that the only respectable professions were the Army, the Navy, the

Church, and possibly other forms of Service to the State, even including politicians. It therefore says a great deal for either Goya's powers of persuasion or his pushfulness that he was able to get the Duke to sit for him. The sitting went far from well! There was no time to paint an elaborate portrait, so Goya made a sketch in sanguine, from which to make a picture later. While he was at work, he interpreted a gesture of his sitter as one of disapproval or contempt and in a fury he reached for a pistol which lay on a table close at hand, whereupon Wellington made to draw his sword, and had it not been for the intervention of friends who were present something dire might have happened, something that could have changed the whole course of European history.

From this sketch Goya painted at least three portraits of the Duke. The original sketch is now preserved in the British Museum, although its natural resting-place would be the National Portrait Gallery. One of the portraits was, until recently, in the possession of the Duke of Leeds, having been given by the Duke to an ancestor of his. Another passed into the possession of the family of General Alava and later formed part of the Havermeyer Collection in New York. The third, which is still in the possession of Wellington's descendants, is an equestrian portrait; concerning this, the following notice appeared in the *Diario de Madrid* on September 1, 1812:

'Starting tomorrow, until the end of the present month, the principal rooms of the Academy of the three noble arts in the Royal Palace will be open to the public; in one of them will be seen the equestrian portrait of Generalissimo Lord Wellington, Duke of Ciudad Rodrigo, which has just been painted by the First Painter to the King and the Director of the Academy, Don Francisco Goya.'

In the opinion of many of the Duke's contemporaries, these were the best portraits of him ever painted. The drawing in the British Museum shows him to be a man of indomitable spirit, but it also reveals the stress and fatigue of his campaigns.

In May 1813, Ferdinand VII, who had passed six years as a virtual prisoner in exile at Valençay in the Department of Indre in the centre of France, returned to Madrid as king, acclaimed as Ferdinand the Desired. And with his return began a reign of terror. All those who had collaborated with Joseph Bonaparte were thrown into prison to await trial for high treason, and Goya only escaped that fate by being given shelter for three months by his friend José Duaso y Latre. When he emerged from hiding he was still a suspected person, but his paintings of the Madrid massacres and some of the *Disasters* that he was able to produce, as well as the fact that he had never worn the 'Egg-plant', were in his favour and he was restored to his old position as First Painter to the King. When he was presented to the new Court the King

Don Quixote:
a drawing by Goya

addressed him thus: 'In our absence you have deserved exile, nay worse, you have merited death; but you are a great artist, and we will forget everything.' In spite of this pardon, Goya was not received into the royal entourage again; he painted a number of portraits of the King, but he never painted any other member of Ferdinand VII's family.

He spent the two years following the Restoration quietly, mostly in drawing, etching, and lithography. It was then that he completed his third and fourth series of etchings, upon which he had been at work at intervals for some years. These were *Tauromaquia* or 'The Art of Bull-fighting' and *Los Disparates*—'The Absurdities' or 'The Stupidities'. Neither of these series was published during his lifetime.

The *Tauromaquia* series traces the history of bull-fighting from the earliest *The Tauromaquia*
times, when bulls were chased and engaged in the open country, until it
developed into the form in which it was practised in Goya's own time, highly
scientifically and in an arena. The original series consisted of thirty-three plates,
which were printed in 1815 under the artist's supervision and issued in a
limited edition for the benefit of a few friends. The public edition, issued by the
Spanish National Engraving Office, did not appear until 1855. In 1876
another edition, with seven extra plates, was issued in France. All these editions
are very rare. The captions under the plates, unlike the enigmatic ones under
the previous series of etchings, are lucidly explanatory, as though the artist were
anxious that their significance should not be missed. They are the least known
of all his etchings, as their appeal, by their very nature, is limited.

A Goya lithograph: *The Divided Arena*

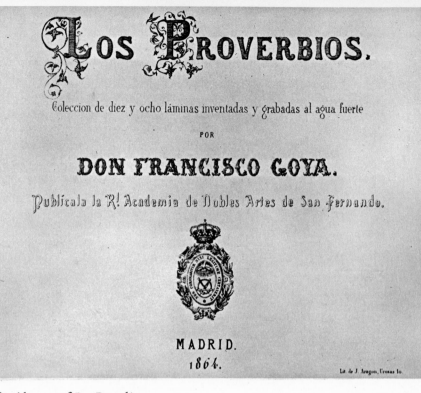

The title-page of *Los Proverbios*

Los Disparates are in a different category altogether. Goya's first title for them was *Los Sueños*—'The Dreams'. They consist of eighteen plates and they are, in a way, a continuation of *Los Caprichos*. They have no captions, however, and one is left to guess at their meaning. They abound in winged monsters, flying men, and horrible grimacing figures. Their title would have been best left as 'Dreams', as there is something thoroughly nightmarish about them, but when they were issued by the Academy of San Fernando long after Goya's death, in 1850, their title was again changed, for no particular reason, to *Los Proverbios*—'The Proverbs'.

Mention has been made of Goya's lithographs. It was only during the second decade of the nineteenth century that he started to experiment with this form, which had only recently been invented. The lithographs are extremely rare, and there is no complete collection in any one place. One of the earliest is of an old woman seated at a spinning-wheel; this is dated February 1819. And there is one in the British Museum which depicts a man being set upon by demons, clearly dating from the time of, and in tune with the spirit of *The Proverbs*.

The Proverbs

Two plates from Goya's *Tauromaquia* on the art of bull-fighting

'The House of the Deaf Man': Goya's country residence outside Madrid

After the Restoration, Goya, who still held the appointment of First Court Painter, realized that his services as such would be no longer required, and he retired to a house he had bought some time before, a little way to the north of Madrid and near the Casa del Campo, a royal hunting-lodge. This house became the rendezvous of all the old friends that were left to him and was known as 'La Quinta del Sordo'—'The House of the Deaf Man'. Here he established himself with a lady who was a distant relative of his, one Doña Leocadia Zorilla Weiss, who had married a German but had been deserted by him. This lady kept house for Francisco and looked after him; she had a strong hold over him in the person of her little daughter, Maria del Rosario, who had been born in 1814, and whom he adored. Indeed, so much did he dote on her that it may well be that she was his own daughter. Leocadia was a shrewish woman, with a bitter tongue, which may account for her husband having left her, but this did not affect Goya, who, being completely deaf, could only understand sign language, and rather primitive sign language at that, and could always take

▲ *Los Proverbios*: men and women dancing to castanets   A cryptic scene from *Los Proverbios* ▼

SS. Justa and Rufina,
one of Goya's
later religious pictures

refuge in feigned incomprehension. Goya was a man to whom feminine com-
panionship was necessary all through his life and Leocadia, though she may
not have been a perfect woman, certainly consoled his declining years, and
remained with him until the end.

Goya was now painting more for his own pleasure than for gain. He refused
to paint portraits except those of his old friends and of people who interested
him. He also painted a number of religious pictures, such as an altarpiece for
Seville Cathedral in 1819, representing Saints Justa and Rufina, two early
Christian Virgins and Martyrs who are often to be found depicted in Spanish
art and are more particularly connected with Seville. He travelled all the way

The Family of Charles IV ▶

*The Last Communion
of Saint Joseph
of Calasanz*

from Madrid to Seville to deliver this picture in person—no mean feat for a deaf and ailing man of over seventy in a country with no proper roads and infested by bandits. And in 1819, also, he painted the picture of *The Last Communion of Saint Joseph of Calasanz* for the Church of San Antonio in the Calle Hortaleza in Madrid. Goya really enjoyed painting this last picture; he himself says that it was a labour of love and he probably put more of himself into it than he had done with any religious picture since his *Holy Family* of over forty years before. It is certainly one of the finest of his compositions. The picture captured his interest because its subject was an Aragonese like himself, and because the church for which it was painted was in the hands of the

*Christ in the
Garden of Olives,*
painted in 1819

Scolope Fathers, who were his first teachers. He painted a picture of Christ in the Garden of Olives and handed that to them also. It still hangs in the Church of San Antonio in Madrid.

Yet a good deal of Goya's time was spent in decorating the interior of his house with grotesque and sometimes diabolical frescoes. In them he gave rein to his natural love of the macabre which had already inspired so many of his etchings. They were mostly painted on the walls of the dining-room on the ground floor and on those of Goya's studio on the floor above. The largest of the paintings, to which Goya did not give a title, but which is known as *The Pilgrimage to the Fountain of San Isidro*, is fifteen feet long and represents a large band of hideous men and women returning drunkenly from their revels and singing uproariously. The fact that it is practically devoid of all colour gives it a nightmarish quality.

*Saturn devouring one of his children,
one of Goya's 'black paintings'*

Two Men fighting with Clubs

The Pilgrimage to the Fountain of San Isidro

The best known and the most horrible of these paintings, entitled *Saturn devouring one of his children*, is too well known to need description. This is closely rivalled by another picture of two men sinking in a quicksand. They are both armed with clubs, and though they know that they have not long to live, they are intent upon fighting one another unto the bitter end, instead of trying to extricate themselves from their predicament. Its message is obvious—the futility of Spaniards fighting each other to the death, in internecine strife, with no thought of anything but the hatred of brother for brother.

After Goya's death the frescoes were removed from the walls: they were shown at the 1878 Paris Exhibition, where they excited frenzied controversy. A well-known contemporary English critic, Philips Gilbert Hamerton, voiced the indignation of those who took offence at the pictures. He said that they 'proved how Goya's mind grovelled in a hideous inferno of its own, a disgusting region, horrible without sublimity, shapeless as chaos, foul in colour and "forlorn of light", peopled by the vilest abortions that ever came from the brain of a sinner. He surrounded himself, I say, with these abominations, finding in

them I know not what devilish satisfaction, and rejoicing, in a manner alto/gether incomprehensible to us, in the audacities of an art in perfect keeping with its revolting subjects. . . . Of all these things the most horrible is the *Saturn*. He is devouring one of his children with the voracity of a famished wolf, and not a detail of the disgusting feast is spared you. The figure is a real inspiration, original as it is terrific, and not a cold product of mere calculating design.'

As a piece of Victorian bluster and diatribe this would be hard to beat, but it is clear that in spite of his indignation Hamerton was impressed with the power of the paintings. They are now all safely housed in the Prado where, from their sombreness of colour and of subjects, they are known as the *pinturas negras*, or 'black paintings'.

The 'Black Paintings'

Goya did not paint many portraits at the House of the Deaf Man, as his relapse in health restricted his activities in that direction; but in 1823 he painted one of his most powerful ones, that of Don Ramon Satué, which is now in the Rijksmuseum in Amsterdam. It shows a firmness of line and touch which is remarkable in a man of his years and bad state of health.

A view of Bordeaux, where Goya spent his last years

Goya leaves Spain In 1824, Goya made up his mind to leave Spain and to seek alleviation of his rheumatic pains elsewhere. He did not, however, wish to abandon his appointment, now purely a nominal one, as First Painter to the Spanish Court, and he obtained six months leave of absence in a document signed by the Grand Chamberlain of the Royal Court, reading as follows: 'Our Lord the King, at the request of the First Court Painter to the Chamber, Don Francisco Goya, has been graciously pleased to grant him His Majesty's royal license to proceed to Plombières in France for the purpose of taking mineral waters in order to alleviate his rheumatism.' This document is dated May 30, and shortly afterwards Goya made his house over to his son Xavier and started out on his travels, but not to Plombières; that was only his excuse for quitting Spain. A fortnight later we hear of him in Bordeaux. It must have been a very uncomfortable journey; travelling in northern Spain and southern France was bad enough on the main routes, but the cross-country trip across the Pyrenees,

Portrait of
Don Ramon Satué,
painted in 1823

mostly by *diligence* over scarcely distinguishable tracks, must have been frightful, particularly for a stone-deaf old man who had practically forgotten all the French he once knew. And as for the inns at which he would have had to put up for the night, they were notorious even in those days for their squalor and lack of sanitation of any kind.

Goya made for Bordeaux because many of his old friends had taken refuge there to escape the wrath of Ferdinand VII and his 'Rehabilitation Tribunal' through which most of the intellectuals and all people suspected of liberalism were made to pass, often into long terms of imprisonment. Chief among Goya's old friends was the poet Don Leandro Fernández de Moratín, and with him he stayed for three days. Moratín pressed him to stay on in Bordeaux, at least for a while, to recover from the fatigues of his journey; but Francisco was anxious to reach Paris, a city which he had always longed to visit, and he arrived there in the early days of June.

He remained in Paris for three months; during his stay he made a number of sketches and painted a couple of portraits of no particular importance. He had promised Moratín to return to Bordeaux before the cold weather set in, and Settles in Bordeaux accordingly he arrived there at the end of September and set up house again with Leocadia Weiss and Maria del Rosario at No. 24 (afterwards altered to 28) Cours de Tourny; it was not, it seems, a very harmonious *ménage*, but Goya, like all deaf people, dreaded loneliness, and Leocadia had become a habit with him; there was also the consolation of the presence of Maria del Rosario, upon whom he still doted.

Meanwhile his six months leave of absence from the Spanish Court expired and he applied for and obtained a prolongation of his leave for the ostensible reason that he wished to try the waters of Bagnères to see if they would do him any more good than those of Plombières had done. But he did not go to Bagnères either!

At about this time he painted a second portrait of Moratín. He had painted him before, in 1799, shortly after their first meeting, and with this earlier portrait, which is one of the best of Goya's great period and now hangs in the Academy of San Fernando, a friendship had begun that lasted for the rest of Goya's life. They were a strangely assorted pair. On the one hand Goya, a man with a peasant upbringing and practically no education, and on the other Moratín, the most important literary figure of his time in Spain, to whom the sound of words was music which meant nothing to the deaf man. Yet theirs was a true and enduring friendship. One can only suppose that Moratín realized what a great artist there was in Goya.

Goya was very restless in Bordeaux and refused to believe that his life was drawing to a close. Moratín, in a letter to a friend, wrote:

'Goya, with his seventy-nine flower-laden years and his perpetual bad health, does not know what he wants or what to hope for. . . . He loves the city [Bordeaux], its surrounding country, its climate, the food, and the independence and quietness which he enjoys there. Since he has been here he has had none of the troubles that used to worry him; yet at times he gets it into his head that he has a great deal to do in Madrid; and if he were allowed to do so, he would set out on a vicious mule, with his hat, his cloak, his wooden stirrups, his wine-skin and his saddle-bags.'

However, he gradually settled down among his old friends exiled from Spain and a few new French ones. On his eightieth birthday he moved into a little house with a north and a south light, No. 10 Rue de la Croix Blanche. Leocadia looked after him, now an impossible termagant, now carefully solicitous of his health. Mariquita, the name by which they called her daughter Maria del Rosario, learned to chatter in French and made friends with the Bordelaises

Goya's signature: a detail from his *Portrait of Don Manuel Osorio de Zuñiga*

of her own age. And, in the quietness of his old age, Goya painted occasional portraits. One of these, which was in the possession of the Comtesse d'Houdetot, was of his friend Jacques Galos, a French business man in Bordeaux who looked after his affairs. On the right of the picture can be faintly traced the words: 'Don Santiago Galos pintado por Goya de edad de 80 años en 1826.' He also painted other portraits in Bordeaux, but the present whereabouts of most of them is unknown, though some are bound to turn up in the course of time.

In May 1826, Goya made a third application for absence from his duties as First Painter to the Spanish Court. This time he had to make the application in person and, in spite of the protests of his friends in Bordeaux, he set off for Madrid. Again we are indebted to Moratín, who, writing to a friend in Spain on May 7 to give him news of the Spanish colony, said:

Revisits Madrid

'One piece of news is Goya's journey to Madrid, which takes place within the next few days. If he has the good fortune not to encounter any trouble on the way, you may greet him on his arrival; if he does not arrive, do not be surprised, as the slightest mishap may leave him dead in a corner of some wayside inn.'

In fact, he arrived safely and, in an interview with the King, obtained from him indefinite leave of absence. The only stipulation that the King made was that Goya should have his portrait painted by Vicente Lopez y Portana, who was the fashionable portrait-painter of the time.

Goya agreed to this. The painting, which is now in the Prado, has been criticized as not having much fire or inspiration; but it is a most conscientious portrait and is quite clearly a striking likeness of the eighty-year-old artist, and does him better justice than many of his own self-portraits. With his impetuous nature he could not be expected not to interfere, and he is said even to have grabbed hold of a brush and started adding a few touches of his own. Lopez was a painter who could never leave a picture alone, always wanting to improve it, but Goya realized this and made the artist stop when he thought the portrait was finished. He then insisted that their respective roles should be reversed and that he should paint Lopez; but nothing seems to have come of this; no such picture is known today.

While in Madrid he took the opportunity of revisiting his old haunts, particularly those where he could contemplate his own work, like the House of the Deaf Man and San Antonio de la Florida, which was particularly dear to his heart because it recalled to him his years of prosperity, good health, and artistic
Back to Bordeaux triumphs. He returned to Bordeaux in July, with his grandson Mariano.

Eager as always for work, Goya was soon back at his drawing-board. He still painted portraits, but they were less ambitious than his early work. The last important portrait he painted was of Don Juan Bautista de Muguiro e Iribarren, an industrialist friend of the artist who had fled from Spain because of his liberal ideas and, like so many other of his compatriots, had taken refuge in Bordeaux. The Muguiro family gave the portrait to the Prado in 1946. It bears the inscription 'Don Juan de Muguiro, by his friend Goya at the age of eighty-one in Bordeaux. May, 1827.' It was at this time, also, that he painted his *La Lechera de Burdeos* ('The Milkmaid of Bordeaux'). His recent portraits had lacked colour and had been almost monochromatic, but the presence of the pretty milkmaid in his studio seems to have rolled back the years and taken him back to the time when he revelled in bright colours. It was the last painting that he finished.

During the last year of his life Goya spent much of his time in a chocolate shop in the Rue de la Petite Taupe, kept by a former citizen of Saragossa, ruined by Spanish politics and now just another refugee. He had learned the trade of chocolate-maker at about the time of the siege of Saragossa in 1808, and his shop was now the regular meeting-place of the other Spanish refugees,

Portrait of Goya at the
age of eighty, painted by
Vicente Lopez y Portana

including Leandro Moratín and Muguiro. Although, owing to his deafness, Goya could not take any active part in the interminable political discussions that went on, he liked to feel that his compatriots whose sympathies he shared were around him. But he would never admit defeat and took a keen interest in the outside world, as can be seen from his letters to his son Xavier. He had moved to the house in which he eventually died, No. 39, now renumbered 57, Cours de l'Indépendence.

Xavier was always on the point of coming to see his father in Bordeaux, but he kept putting it off, and Goya was left with Leocadia, the little fourteen-year-old Rosario and his grandson Mariano, now a young man. However, in response to an urgent message from Mariano, Xavier arrived in Bordeaux early in April 1828. On the fifteenth of that month Goya was stricken with apoplexy and became unconscious. He died next morning without regaining conscious- *Death* ness, at the age of eighty-two. His son, his grandson, Leocadia Weiss, and Rosario were at his bedside.

Goya was interred in a vault where the remains of a connexion of his by marriage had been placed three years before. Seventy-two years later, in May 1900, his remains were removed to Madrid, where they were buried in the cemetery of San Isidro, beside those of his old friend the poet Leandro Moratín.

Goya lived at a time when the whole of Spain was in a state of havoc and chaos, and it says a great deal for his indomitable courage and strength of character that he was able to rise above all the difficulties that beset him. His main claim to greatness is that, having discovered his own technique and style, he refused to follow any school slavishly. He painted to please himself except on the occasions when he was commanded, in his capacity as First Painter to the Court, to paint people in whom he had no interest. He was the forerunner of the Romantic movement in art that started within a few years of his death and on which his paintings had so much influence. Apart from anything else, he has handed down to us a brilliantly informative picture of the Spain of his day.

On the house in which Goya died in Bordeaux there is an inscription carved on a stone slab, set high in the wall, which reads:

FRANCISCO GOYA Y LUCIENTES
né a Fuendetodos (Espagne)
le 30 Mars 1746
est mort dans cette maison
le 16 Avril 1828

For all that this tells us, the man whose name it commemorates might be some local dignitary who happened to be born away from his home town; there is no mention at all of the fact that Goya was one of the greatest artists that the world has produced.

Goya's tomb at Bordeaux

1746 Francisco José Goya y Lucientes was born at No. 18 Calle de Alfóndiga, Fuendetodos, in the province of Saragossa on March 30. He was the son of José Goya, by profession a gilder, and his wife Engracia, *née* Lucientes, a lady of *hidalgo* descent.

1749 The Goya family moves to the city of Saragossa and establishes itself in the Calle de la Morería Cerrada. It was during the following few years that the young Goya was placed under the instruction of José Luzan y Martinez, the foremost art master in Saragossa at that time.

1765 Goya moves to Madrid, possibly to avoid complications arising from his escapades in Saragossa.

1769 Finding things getting awkward also in Madrid, Goya makes for Italy, to study the great classical pictures of the Renaissance.

1771 Precipitate departure of Goya from Rome, following a romantic attempt upon an inmate of a convent.

1772 Goya awarded second prize in a competition held by the Royal Academy of Fine Arts at Parma. Goya commissioned to paint frescoes for the Cathedral of El Pilar in Saragossa.

1775 Goya marries his patron and teacher's sister, Josefa Bayeu, who was to bear him twenty children, only one of whom, Xavier, survived him.

1776 Goya starts work on the cartoons for the tapestries for the Royal Tapestry Factory at Santa Bárbara.

1779 Elected to the Royal Academy of San Fernando.

1780 Resumes work on the Cathedral of El Pilar. This came to nothing.

1781 Death of Goya's father in December.

1784 Goya paints an altarpiece for the Church of San Francisco el Grande. This was unveiled by King Charles III in December and first set Goya's foot on the ladder of success. From this year dates his friendship with the King's brother, the Infante Don Luis. He painted many portraits of the family and was commissioned to paint many pictures to adorn the Infante's palace.

1785 Goya appointed Assistant Director of the Academy of San Fernando. In the same year painted the famous portrait of the Count of Floridablanca.

1786 Appointed official painter to the Royal Tapestry factory.

1788 Death of Charles III; accession of Charles IV and appointment of Goya to position of Court Painter.

1789 Meeting of Goya and the Duchess of Alba and the start of their great romance.

1793 Banishment of the Duchess of Alba to her estates near Sanlúcar. Goya follows her and refuses to return to Madrid without her. The Duchess recalled in the following year, this being the only way to get Goya back to the capital.

1795 Goya resigns from his appointment as official painter to the Royal Tapestry Factory.

Chronology

1798 Starts work on one of the principal monuments to his fame, the decorations of the Church of San Antonio de la Florida.

1799 Appointed First Court Painter.

1800 Paints the family group of King Charles IV, now in the Prado. About the same time, paints the two *Majas*, also in the Prado.

1801 Paints the portrait of Godoy that now hangs in the Academy of San Fernando in Madrid.

1803 First general issue of *The Caprichos*.

1808 The two paintings *The Second of May* and *The Third of May*, depicting the Madrid massacres, date from this year.

1810 *The Disasters of War* etched, but not published until after Goya's death.

1812 Josefa, Goya's wife, dies. Goya paints the Duke of Wellington.

1813 The series of bull-fighting etchings and *Los Disparates*, or 'The Absurdities', date from this year, and were first published in a very limited edition in 1815.

1819 Goya starts experimenting with the newly invented art of lithography. At about the same time he retires to the house just outside Madrid known as *La Quinta del Sordo*—The House of the Deaf Man, which he proceeds to decorate with a series of weird and sometimes horrific frescoes. These have now been removed to the Prado.

1824 Goya leaves Spain to go to Bordeaux, on his way to Paris, where he remains for three months, before returning to Bordeaux to be near his old friend Leandro de Moratín.

1826 Goya pays his last visit to Madrid, to obtain indefinite leave of absence from the Court, which as First Court Painter he must do. It was at this time that the well-known portrait of him by Vicente Lopez y Portana was painted.

1827 Goya paints his last portrait, that of Don Juan Bautista de Muguiro e Irabarren, in May. In this year he also paints his last finished picture, *The Milkmaid of Bordeaux*, one of the most touching of all his paintings, which shows that his admiration of feminine beauty remained with him until the end.

1828 Death of Goya on April 16 at No. 39 Cours de l'Indépendence, Bordeaux, surrounded by all that was left of his family, at the age of eighty-two. He was interred in Bordeaux.

1900 Goya's remains are removed to Madrid.

NOTES ON THE PICTURES

Page numbers with an asterisk refer to a colour plate on the facing page

Frontispiece. A SELF-PORTRAIT OF GOYA at the age of sixty-nine, painted in 1815. Prado Museum, Madrid. *Photo Anderson*

Page

5 SARAGOSSA is the capital city of the Province of Aragon in which Goya was born, and where he first started to paint at the age of fifteen. From Charles Yriarte's *Goya*, Paris, 1867. *Photo Thames and Hudson Archives*

7 GOYA'S BIRTHPLACE. A modern photograph of the house which is still standing. *Photo Mas, Barcelona*

8 SARAGOSSA was renowned for its churches and miracle-working relics. This photograph shows the famous Cathedral of El Pilar by the River Ebro; it was the rival church to the Cathedral of La Seo. *Photo Thames and Hudson Archives*

9 MARTIN ZAPATER was Goya's first and closest friend, ever since they both went to school together. They corresponded frequently over a period of many years. The portrait reproduced was painted by Goya in 1797. Its present location is unknown. *Photo Thames and Hudson Archives*

10 SARAGOSSA. From an early-nineteenth-century print. *By courtesy of the Courtauld Institute of Art, London*

11 SARAGOSSA. Cathedral of La Seo. This fine Gothic church was twin-cathedral with El Pilar. Each church had its own special festivals and processions which sometimes led to clashes between the rival bands of

parishioners. Engraving from E. H. Locker's *Views of Spain*, 1824. *By courtesy of the Trustees of the British Museum. Photo Thames and Hudson Archives*

12 THE ALTARPIECE AT FUENDETODOS. The paintings on the two wing-panels and on the walls above are traditionally attributed to Goya and are probably the earliest examples we have of his work, painted during his adolescence. *Photo Mas, Barcelona*

13 MADRID, the Street of San Bernardo. An engraving by James Allen from a drawing by David Roberts. Goya first came to the city in 1765. *By courtesy of the Courtauld Institute of Art, London*

14 GOYA. A self-portrait painted *c.* 1772–4 when the artist was in his late twenties. *By courtesy of the City Art Museum, St Louis*

15 THE APPARITION OF THE VIRGIN OF THE PILLAR, painted by Goya for the Church of Fuendetodos. This may date from 1772–4 when Goya was engaged in painting frescoes for the Cathedral of El Pilar. *Photo Mas, Barcelona*

16 ANTON RAPHAEL MENGS (1728–79) was the First Painter to the Spanish Court at the time that Goya first came to Madrid, and the acknowledged leader of painting in Spain. He became a good friend to Goya and greatly helped him at the start of his career. From G. L. Bianconi, *Elogio Storico del Cavaliere Anton Raffaele Mengs*, Milan, 1780. *By courtesy of the Trustees of the British Museum. Photo Thames and Hudson Archives*

17 'UNA CALLE' in Madrid, one of the rare topographical drawings by Goya. Prado Museum, Madrid. *Photo Mas, Barcelona*

18 THE ESCORIAL was the palace built by Philip II as a place where he might pass his last years in quiet and religious devotions. It now houses some of the royal tapestries for which Goya painted his famous cartoons, and many other works of art. It is also the last resting-place of the kings of Spain from Charles V onwards. Engraving from E. H. Locker's *Views of Spain*, 1824. *By courtesy of the Trustees of the British Museum. Photo Thames and Hudson Archives*

ARANJUEZ. THE ROYAL PALACE. This was the summer residence of the later Bourbon kings of Spain. Situated only a few miles south-east of Madrid, it was famous for its picture collection and its magnificent gardens, laid out by Charles IV before he came to the throne. It was his favourite home. Engraving from Laborde's *Itinéraire déscriptif de l'Espagne*, Paris, 1834. *By courtesy of the Trustees of the British Museum. Photo Thames and Hudson Archives*

19 THE DUEL. Goya lived in violent, dangerous times. During his turbulent youth he may well have witnessed the scene he portrays here. The picture is in the Alte Pinakothek, Munich. *Photo Mansell Collection*

20 ROME. The Square of St Peter's. This view is from an anonymous eighteenth-century painting of *The Papal Benediction*, now in the Borghese Collection, Rome. *Photograph by the Gabinetto Fotografico Nazionale, Ministero dell' Istruzione Pubblica, Rome*

21 A VIEW OF ROME that Goya knew. From an etching by Piranesi in his series *Vedute di Roma*. 1748–78. *By courtesy of the Royal Institute of British Architects*

23 LA FÉ, a detail of one of the frescoes that Goya painted for the Cathedral of El Pilar in Saragossa shortly after his return from Italy in 1772. This was Goya's first important commission. *Photo Mas, Barcelona*

24 THIS FRESCO is on one of the vaults of the Cathedral of El Pilar, Saragossa, painted by Goya. *Photo Mas, Barcelona*

25 THE HOLY FAMILY, painted in 1784. This is probably the most charming of all Goya's pictures on sacred themes. He was not a 'religious' artist by temperament: his *Holy Family* is really a study of domesticity taken from everyday life. Prado Museum, Madrid. *Photo Anderson*

26 THE AULA DEI was a monastic institution a few miles to the north of Saragossa, where Goya received a commission to paint a series of frescoes *c.* 1772–4, mainly devoted to scenes from the life of the Virgin. The building was badly damaged during the Peninsular War and many of the frescoes were ruined. *Photo Mas, Barcelona*

27 Goya painted this *Crucifixion* very soon after his return from Italy in 1771. The painting is now in the Prado Museum, Madrid. *Photo Anderson*

28 GOYA'S WIFE was the sister of his teacher Bayeu. The painting is now in the Prado Museum, Madrid. *Photo Anderson*

29 FRANCISCO BAYEU. Goya painted this portrait in 1786 to seal their reconciliation after a quarrel about the frescoes in the Cathedral of El Pilar, Saragossa. Museo San Carlos, Valencia. *Photo Mas, Barcelona*

30 THE BULL-FIGHT. Goya was a lifelong *aficionado*, a devotee of the bull-ring and a friend of many of the bull-fighters of his day. The illustration is from Plate 20 of his *Tauromaquia* series of etchings and is entitled *Quickness and dexterity of Juanito Apiñani in the Madrid ring*. From the collection of Tomas Harris. *Photo by courtesy of the Witt Library, Courtauld Institute of Art*

31 JOSÉ ROMERO, THE BULL-FIGHTER. This is one of Goya's most outstanding portraits, painted in 1810. Collection of Mrs Carroll S. Tyson, Chestnut Hill, Philadelphia, Pa.

32 BLIND MAN'S BUFF was painted by Goya early in 1787. In 1786 he was appointed painter to the Royal Tapestry Factory and designed cartoons for tapestries. Prado Museum, Madrid. *Photo Anderson*

33 THE VINTAGE by Goya. The picture reproduced is one of a series entitled *The Four Seasons*, and is in the Prado Museum, Madrid. *Photo Anderson*

34 THE STILT-WALKERS was painted by Goya in 1791–2 for a tapestry. Charles III, the King of Spain, had asked that the subjects for the tapestries should be taken from the daily life of the Spanish people. Prado Museum, Madrid. *Photo Mas, Barcelona*

35 THE CROCKERY SELLER, painted by Goya in 1779 as a tapestry design, shows a wayside crockery seller displaying her wares on the ground for the attention of passers-by. Prado Museum, Madrid. *Photo Mas, Barcelona*

36 DON JUAN ANTONIO CUERVO. Goya had for long been connected with the Royal Academy of San Fernando, being elected in 1780, and appointed President in 1785. In 1819 he painted Cuervo, an architect, who was then Director of the Academy. H. Marlatt Collection, Museum of Art, Cleveland

37 THE PRADO, in Madrid, where the famous Museum is now situated, was a wide avenue and one of the most popular resorts for the people of eighteenth-century Madrid. It was chosen as the site for a national museum by order of King Charles III. From Laborde's *Itinéraire déscriptif de l'Espagne*, Paris, 1834. *By courtesy of the Trustees of the British Museum. Photo Thames and Hudson Archives*

38 MARIA LUISA as Princess of Parma before she married the Spanish Infante (later Charles IV). The portrait, which forms an interesting contrast to that reproduced on page 39 is by Raphael Mengs, one of Goya's first and most influential friends in the art world at the time he came to Madrid. Prado Museum, Madrid. *Photo Anderson*

39 MARIA LUISA, wife of Charles IV of Spain, was notorious for her liaison with Manuel Godoy, her wilful temperament and her sensuality. Despite the unflattering honesty of Goya's portrait painted when she was in her late thirties, she was to commission others, and remained a steady admirer of his work. Palazzo Reale di Capodimonte, Naples. *Photo Alinari*

40 GOYA was always interested in experimenting and in learning new techniques. In about 1775 he turned his hand to etching and made a series of copies after Velazquez, whom he greatly admired, and whose paintings he was able to see in Madrid. The etching reproduced is after Velazquez's equestrian portrait of Don Balthasar Carlos, now in the Prado. Garrett Collection, The Baltimore Museum of Art

41 THE FLAGELLANTS is one of Goya's studies of the religious fanaticism that persisted so strongly in Spain in the late eighteenth century. Such religious processions in which penitents publicly scourged themselves were no uncommon sight in Goya's day. Academy of San Fernando, Madrid. *Photo Mas, Barcelona*

43 THE VIRGIN AS QUEEN OF THE MARTYRS. A sketch for one of the frescoes that Goya was commissioned to paint for the Cathedral of El Pilar in Saragossa in 1780, now in the Diocesan Museum of the Cathedral of La Seo. *Photo Mas, Barcelona*

44 SARAGOSSA. A view of the city from a print made during Goya's lifetime. From Laborde's *Voyage pittoresque et historique de l'Espagne*, 1806–20. *By courtesy of the Trustees of the British Museum. Photo Thames and Hudson Archives*

45 GOYA'S WORK for the Cathedral in Saragossa led to a bitter quarrel with Francisco Bayeu, his brother-in-law, and with the Cathedral authorities who considered Goya's designs as being too modern in spirit, and the colouring too dark. Diocesan Museum, Cathedral of La Seo, Saragossa. *Photo Mas, Barcelona*

46 THE PUERTA DEL SOL, situated in the centre of Madrid, was the site of the Town Hall and the meeting-place of all Madrid. It was here that Napoleon's Mamelukes cut down the city's inhabitants during the 1808 uprising. From Laborde's *Voyage pittoresque et historique de l'Espagne*, 1806–20. *By courtesy of the Trustees of the British Museum. Photo Thames and Hudson Archives*

47 GOYA'S PORTRAIT OF AN OLD LADY is said to be a picture of his mother. Goya seems to have fought shy of painting his parents as there are no other portraits of them in existence. *By courtesy of the Berlin-Dahlem Museum. Photo by Walter Steinkopf*

48 SAN BERNARDIN OF SIENA was painted by Goya in 1784 for one of the altarpieces of the new Church of San Francisco el Grande in Madrid, and was one of his most painstaking efforts. The picture shows the Saint preaching from a rock to King Alfonso of Aragon. Now in the Collection of the Count of Villagonzalo. *Photo Mas, Barcelona*

49 THE INFANTE DON LUIS OF BOURBON was one of Goya's closest friends in the Royal Family. He had been made Cardinal as a child, but later renounced the office, and was permitted to marry the beautiful Doña Maria Teresa de Vallabriga, the daughter of an old Aragon family, and retired to his estates in

Castile. Goya has included himself in the bottom left-hand corner of the picture. In the Collection of the Duke of Sueca. *Photo Mas, Barcelona*

50 GOYA'S PORTRAIT OF CHARLES III was painted shortly before the King's death in 1788. The composition of the picture is very similar to that of Velazquez's *Philip IV*, in the Prado, where there is another copy by Goya of the picture here reproduced. Museo Municipal, Madrid. *Photo Mas, Barcelona*

51 GOYA'S PORTRAIT of the Infante Don Luis Antonio de Bourbon, brother of Charles III and patron of the artist. Private Collection. *Photo Mas, Barcelona*

52 THE PORTRAIT OF COUNTESS CHINCHÓN as a child is one of Goya's most appealing works. He had known the Countess as a little girl, when he was painting the family of her father, the Infante Don Luis. She was later to marry Manuel Godoy. Private Collection. *Photo Mas, Barcelona*

53 MARIA TERESA DE VALLABRIGA was renowned for her beauty. This portrait was painted by Goya during his stay at the Infante Don Luis's estates at Las Arenas de San Pedro in Castile in the summer of 1783. Private Collection. *Photo Mas, Barcelona*

54 THE CITY ON A ROCK was painted by Goya *c.* 1815. Its meaning is cryptic: in its spirit it has close affinities with some of his etched work, the winged men flying in the right-hand corner of the picture are a theme which recurs in his late etchings, *Los Proverbios*. *By courtesy of the Metropolitan Museum of Art, New York*

55 THE CARDINAL DON LUIS MARIA of Bourbon and Vallabriga was the son of the Infante Don Luis. He became Archbishop of Toledo, Primate of Spain. Prado Museum, Madrid. *Photo Mas, Barcelona*

57 THE COUNT OF FLORIDABLANCA was Charles III's powerful Prime Minister and one of the few real statesmen in Spain at the time. When Charles IV came to the throne, the Count's place was taken by Godoy: he was ignominiously dismissed and imprisoned. The figure on the left is a self-portrait of Goya. Collection of the Marqués de Valdueza. *Photo Mas, Barcelona*

58 THE CALLE ALCALÁ was one of the few broad thoroughfares running through the old city of Madrid, with its dark, narrow streets that Goya used to roam during his adventurous youth. Engraving by J. T. Wilmore from a drawing by David Roberts, London, 1836. *By courtesy of the Courtauld Institute of Art*

59 THE OSUNA FAMILY is one of the oldest and noblest in Spain. The Duchess of Osuna became an admirer of Goya's work and one of his most powerful patrons. From Charles Yriarte's *Goya*, Paris, 1867. *By courtesy of the Trustees of the British Museum. Photo Thames and Hudson Archives*

60 THE PICNIC was one of Goya's pictures which was owned by his patron the Duke of Osuna. It was painted in 1776. *By courtesy of the Trustees, the National Gallery, London*

61 GOYA became friendly with the ducal family of Osuna some time in 1785. The most important member of the family was the Duchess, who had married her cousin, the Duke. She was famous for her wealth, her love of the arts, and her unconventional behaviour. She gave Goya many important commissions. The picture was given to the Prado Museum in 1890 by descendants of the family. *Photo Anderson*

62 THE PILGRIMAGE OF SAN ISIDRO was held on a very popular feast-day in Madrid, on May 15 every year, when the city populace would cross the River Manzanares to gather in the meadows outside the city. Prado Museum, Madrid. *Photo Anderson*

63 THE CONVENT OF SAN ISIDRO, the focal-point of the Festival, was situated in the outskirts of Madrid. It was here that the inhabitants of Madrid made their devotions to the Saint. From Laborde's *Voyage pittoresque et historique de l'Espagne*, 1806–20. *By courtesy of the Trustees of the British Museum. Photo Thames and Hudson Archives*

65 THE MARQUESA DE PONTEJOS, subject of one of Goya's most elegant portraits, was a sister-in-law of the Count of Floridablanca. She was one of the most fashionable women in Madrid society and followed the French mode. *By courtesy of the National Gallery of Art, Washington D.C., Mellon Collection*

66 CHARLES IV (1748–1819) was a weak-willed man who was content to hand over the reins of government to the Queen and her lover Godoy. Under pressure from Napoleon he abdicated in 1807. This portrait is one of several that Goya painted and is in the Palazzo Reale di Capodimonte, Naples. *Photo Alinari*

67 MARIA LUISA, wife of Charles IV. Another portrait of the Queen, painted in 1790, now in the Prado Museum. *Photo Anderson*

68 ALTHOUGH Godoy's political influence was, in the main, disastrous, he was a good friend to Goya and a generous patron. This portrait was painted in 1801 and is in the Academy of San Fernando, Madrid. *Photo Anderson*

68*THE PARASOL was painted by Goya in 1777 and is one of his earliest 'cartoons' for the Royal Tapestry Factory at Madrid. Prado Museum, Madrid.

69 VALENCIA, where Goya was elected a member of the Academy of San Carlos. From Laborde's *Voyage pittoresque et historique de l'Espagne*, 1806–20. *By courtesy of the Trustees of the British Museum. Photo Thames and Hudson Archives*

70 THIS FAMOUS PORTRAIT of the Duchess of Alba was painted by Goya in 1795 and is in the Liria Palace in Madrid, in the Collection of the present Duke of Alba. *Photo Mas, Barcelona*

71 A PORTRAIT of the Duchess of Alba's infant son, painted by Goya. *By courtesy of the Frick Collection, New York*

72 A DETAIL from a portrait of the Duchess of Alba that Goya painted in 1797, showing the rings marked 'Alba' and 'Goya'. Metropolitan Museum of Art. *By courtesy of the Hispanic Society of America, New York*

73 THE DUCHESS OF ALBA. This is the most famous of the several portraits that Goya painted of the Duchess. *By courtesy of the Hispanic Society of America, New York*

75 GOYA AND THE DUCHESS OF ALBA. This picture, painted in 1793, is now in the Collection of the Marquess de la Romana, Madrid. Goya is shown as a youthful dandy, and the Duchess as wearing typical *maja* costume of the period. *Photo Mas, Barcelona*

76 THE DREAM OF LIES AND INCONSTANCY. Plate 81 of *Los Caprichos*. This engraving is one of three plates Goya added later to the series. *Photo Thames and Hudson Archives*

76*THE CLOTHED MAJA is the companion picture to *The Naked Maja* and painted at the same time. The date of the two pictures is uncertain, being usually put at *c.* 1797–8. Prado Museum, Madrid.

77 THIS PAINTING by Goya gives us a good idea of the typical costume of the period worn by the Spanish lower classes. The flamboyant costume worn by the *maja* greatly appealed to the aristocratic ladies of the time, who often used to wear it out of affectation. Samuel H. Kress Collection, Museum of Fine Arts of Houston, Houston, Texas

78 THIS DRAWING is one of many that Goya made during his stay at Sanlúcar with the Duchess of Alba in 1793–4 when he filled up a sketch-book with drawings made on the spot. The lady in the sketch is popularly supposed to be the Duchess herself. Prado Museum, Madrid. *Photo Anderson*

79 THE NAKED MAJA. The old myth that the Duchess of Alba herself posed for this celebrated picture is no longer given any credit. The astonishing thing about the picture, though, is that it should even have been painted, as the representation of nudity was virtually prohibited in Spain by the Inquisition which was still powerful in Goya's time. Prado Museum, Madrid. *Photo Anderson*

80 IN 1795, after the death of Goya's brother-in-law, Francisco Bayeu, the post of First Court Painter became vacant, and Goya sent a petition to the King asking for the post. Although he was supported in his request by Godoy, it was not granted until 1799. The illustration shows a copy of the report on the King's first refusal. British Museum, Egerton MS. 586, f. 73. *By courtesy of the Trustees of the British Museum*

81 LOS CAPRICHOS, Plate 26, is a satire directed against Woman's vanity. Goya's own written comments to the picture are 'In order to make featherbrained girls settle down, the best thing is to put a chair on their heads.' Tomas Harris Collection. *Photo by courtesy of the Witt Library, Courtauld Institute of Art*

TO HIS GRANDFATHER. Plate 39 of *Los Caprichos*. This plate is generally taken to be a satire on Godoy, who was obsessed with proving his own noble ancestry. Goya's commentary is 'This poor animal has been driven mad by genealogists and heralds. He is not the only one.' Tomas Harris Collection. *Photo by courtesy of the Witt Library, Courtauld Institute of Art*

82 CORRECTION. Plate 46 of *Los Caprichos*. This picture is one of a set in *Los Caprichos* devoted to representation of sorcery, which was still practised in Spain during Goya's lifetime. He comments: '. . . Witchcraft requires a particular talent, application, maturity, submission and docility to the advice from the great Wizard. . . .' Tomas Harris Collection. *Photo by courtesy of the Witt Library, Courtauld Institute of Art*

83 A MEETING OF THE SPANISH INQUISITION, painted by Goya. He painted several scenes of the Inquisition holding its tribunals which were still a frequent occurrence in late-eighteenth-century Spain, although the terrible *autos-da-fé* were no longer held. Goya himself risked prosecution by the Inquisition more than once. Although it was abolished by Joseph Bonaparte in 1807 it was restored in 1814 by the reactionary Ferdinand VII. Academy of San Fernando, Madrid. *Photo Anderson*

84 THE CHURCH OF SAN ANTONIO DE LA FLORIDA in Madrid that Goya decorated by order of King Charles IV in 1798. *Photo by courtesy of the Courtauld Institute of Art*

85 PART OF GOYA'S FRESCO DECORATIONS in the cupola of San Antonio de la Florida, showing Saint Anthony of Padua raising a dead man to life. *Photo Mas, Barcelona*

86 THE CUPOLA OF SAN ANTONIO DE LA FLORIDA. Detail of Goya's fresco decoration showing some of the many life-size figures modelled from members of the fashionable Madrid society of the period. *Photo Mas, Barcelona*

87 THIS SELF-PORTRAIT was painted when Goya was First Painter to the King, and some three years after his illness which resulted in his total deafness. The painting is now in the Musée Bonnat, Bayonne. *Archives Photographiques, Paris*

88 THE INFANTA MARIA JOSEFA, a sketch made by Goya *c.* 1799 for his famous portrait of Charles IV and his family. She was the eldest daughter of Charles III. Prado Museum, Madrid. *Photo Mas, Barcelona*

89 THE INFANTE DON FRANCISCO DE PAULA ANTONIO. Another study by Goya for his group portrait of the Royal Family. The little boy was the younger son of Charles IV, although it was widely rumoured that his real father was Manuel Godoy, whose affair with the Queen was current knowledge. Prado Museum, Madrid. *Photo Mas, Barcelona*

90 GOYA'S STUDIO. This imaginary scene, with the painter standing by a huge canvas while his friends dance to castanets, was painted by Francisco Domingo y Marqués (1842–1920). *By courtesy of the Hispanic Society of America, New York*

91 FERDINAND GUILLEMARDET was the French Republic's Ambassador to the Court of Spain in 1798. He commissioned Goya to paint his portrait which he took back to France with him. In 1865 it was acquired from his descendants by the Louvre, where it may be seen today. *Archives Photographiques, Paris*

92 DOÑA ANTONIA ZARATE was a well-known actress in Madrid who was to die from consumption at an early age. The date of Goya's portrait of her is uncertain; it may have been 1805. Alfred Beit Collection, Blessington, Ireland. *Photo Mas, Barcelona*

93 FRANCISCO XAVIER GOYA was Goya's only surviving child. Goya was very proud of his son and obtained a royal pension for him. He worked as an art student for a time, but inherited none of his father's talent. In this portrait, now in a private collection, he is shown in the costume of an elegant dandy of the period. *Photo Anc. Coll. Vizzavona-Druet, Musées Nationaux*

94 FERDINAND VII, son of Charles IV, became king after the abdication of his father during the French invasion. He was later imprisoned by Napoleon and finally restored to the throne in 1814. On his return to Spain he re-established the Inquisition and instituted a merciless persecution of his political opponents, in particular the Spanish liberals. Thyssen-Bornemisza Collection. *Reproduced by courtesy of the owners*

95 THE DISASTERS OF WAR, Plate 50. One of the tragic incidents of war: men carry away the dead body of a woman while her little child looks on in tears. Tomas Harris Collection. *Photo by courtesy of the Witt Library, Courtauld Institute of Art*

96 EPISODE OF THE SECOND OF MAY, 1808. This and the following one are two of Goya's most famous paintings, now in the Prado Museum. Goya was in Madrid at the time of the city's rising against Murat's French troops and may well have been an eyewitness of the appalling massacre that took place in the Puerta del Sol. *By courtesy of the Spanish National Tourist Office, London*

97 THE THIRD OF MAY, 1808. Spanish prisoners who have been taken during the rising are being mercilessly shot down outside the city walls, one of the many heavy reprisals carried out by the French. Prado Museum, Madrid. *Photo Anderson*

98 THIS LAST SELF-PORTRAIT by Goya was painted *c.* 1826, probably at Bordeaux, a year before his death. *Photo by courtesy of Kunsthistorisches Museum, Vienna*

99 ONE OF TWO PAINTINGS in which Goya shows the Spanish guerrillas at work in the forests of the Spanish sierra, making gunpowder and bullets in order to carry on the struggle against the French. *Photo Mas, Barcelona*

101 THE ALLEGORY OF THE CITY OF MADRID was painted by Goya in 1810, being commissioned by the Municipal Council of Madrid. Originally the marble plaque held by the angels contained a portrait of Joseph Bonaparte which was later changed to the word 'Constitución'; for this a portrait of Ferdinand VII was next substituted, only to be replaced finally by the inscription 'Dos de Mayo' to commemorate the rising of the city in 1808 against the French. The picture is still in the Madrid Town Hall, its original destination. *Photo Mas, Barcelona*

102 A WOMAN ATTACKED BY BRIGANDS by Goya. Such scenes were a common feature in Spain during the Peninsular War. The whole country was ravaged by marauding bandits and guerrillas who often attacked both friend and foe alike. Collection of Dr Carvalho. *Photo Giraudon*

103 GENERAL JUAN MARTÍN, nicknamed 'El Empecinado', was the peasant son of a cobbler who became the most famous guerrilla leader in Spain. He entered Madrid with Wellington in 1812 in triumphal procession at the head of the Spanish troops. Under Ferdinand VII he was imprisoned and later executed. Private Collection, Venezuela. *Photo Mas, Barcelona*

104 THE DISASTERS OF WAR, Plate 31. A French soldier is sheathing his sword; in the background two other soldiers are bending over a woman, while a dead Spaniard hangs from a tree. Tomas Harris Collection. *Photo by courtesy of the Witt Library, Courtauld Institute of Art*

105 THE DISASTERS OF WAR. Plate 43. A view of Spanish monks fleeing from the enemy, who are probably pillaging their monastery. Tomas Harris Collection. *Photo by courtesy of the Witt Library, Courtauld Institute of Art*

105 THE DISASTERS OF WAR. Plate 45. Men, women, and children, carrying their household belongings, flee from the terrors of war —a tragic, timeless scene, as seen by Goya. Tomas Harris Collection. *Photo by courtesy of the Witt Library, Courtauld Institute of Art*

106 ALTHOUGH Goya etched *The Disasters of War* between 1810 and 1813, the first edition of the series was not published until 1863 by the Academy of San Fernando. Tomas Harris Collection. *Photo by courtesy of the Witt Library, Courtauld Institute of Art*

107 GOYA MET THE DUKE OF WELLINGTON in 1812 when the Duke liberated Madrid at the head of the Anglo-Spanish army. Goya was commissioned to paint the General, and this sketch in red chalk is a study for the finished portrait. *By courtesy of the Trustees of the British Museum*

109 THE DUKE OF WELLINGTON ON HORSEBACK. Goya painted two portraits of the Duke, one half-length, and the other one on horseback, as reproduced here. In September 1812 the picture was put on public exhibition in the Royal Academy in Madrid. It is now in Apsley House, London, the home of the present Duke. *By courtesy of the Victoria and Albert Museum, London. Crown Copyright*

110 DON QUIXOTE, a drawing by Goya now in the British Museum, London. In spirit, the sketch is somewhat reminiscent of some of *Los Caprichos. By courtesy of the Trustees of the British Museum,*

111 TO THE VERY END OF HIS LIFE GOYA was always ready to experiment with new techniques. He became interested in the newly invented process of lithography, and produced several striking works in this medium. The picture is a scene from a bullfight: the arena has been divided into two halves so that simultaneous combats may take place. *By courtesy of the Rijksmuseum, Amsterdam*

112 LOS PROVERBIOS: title-page of the 1864 edition. The original title that Goya gave to this series of etchings was *Los Sueños* ('The Dreams'). They were not published until many years after his death. The title-page reproduced here is for the second edition published by the Academy of San Fernando in 1864. Tomas Harris Collection. *Photo by courtesy of the Witt Library, Courtauld Institute of Art*

113 THE TAUROMAQUIA. Plate 1: Goya's title for the plate is *Method of the Ancient Spaniards of chasing bulls in the open on horseback.* The series, which Goya had printed in 1815, was intended to show the origins and development of the art of bull-fighting. The first edition was not put on sale until after the artist's death. Tomas Harris Collection. *Photo by courtesy of the Witt Library, Courtauld Institute of Art*

THE TAUROMAQUIA. Plate 28: *The brave Rendon spearing a bull which he kills with a blow, in the Madrid ring.* Rendon was one of the most celebrated bull-fighters of the time, and Goya must have seen him fight when he came to Madrid. Tomas Harris Collection. *Photo by courtesy of the Witt Library, Courtauld Institute of Art*

114 SHORTLY AFTER Ferdinand VII's restoration, Goya left Madrid to take up residence in a small two-storey house outside the city by the River Manzanares, which became known as 'The House of the Deaf Man'. From Charles Yriarte's *Goya*, Paris, 1867. *By courtesy of the Trustees of the British Museum. Photo Thames and Hudson Archives*

115 LOS PROVERBIOS. Plate 12: three men and three women with grotesque, mask-like faces dance to castanets. They are wearing typical *majo* and *maja* costume. Tomas Harris Collection. *Photo by courtesy of the Witt Library, Courtauld Institute of Art*

115 LOS PROVERBIOS. Plate 8: men dressed in sacks, bowing respectfully before a leader whom they follow in procession. The picture has been taken to show men's slavery to convention. Tomas Harris Collection. *Photo by courtesy of the Witt Library, Courtauld Institute of Art*

116 SS. JUSTA AND RUFINA, sketch for an altarpiece painted by Goya for Seville Cathedral in 1817. As models for these early Christian martyrs he took two ladies renowned for their light morals. Prado Museum, Madrid. *Photo Mas, Barcelona*

116*THE FAMILY OF CHARLES IV. This is Goya's most successful and famous group portrait. It was painted at the royal summer palace in Aranjuez in the spring of 1800 shortly after Goya had obtained the coveted post of First Painter to the King. Goya himself appears in the picture, facing his easel in the extreme left of the picture. Prado Museum, Madrid.

117 SAINT JOSEPH OF CALASANZ was a saint of Goya's native province of Aragon. He lived to an extremely old age and at the end of his life he had himself taken to church every day at the time the local school-children were hearing Mass. In 1819 Goya was commissioned to paint this picture by the Scolope Fathers of Madrid, whose Order had been founded by the Saint. The picture is in the Church of San Antonio in Madrid. *Photo Mas, Barcelona*

118 ANOTHER of Goya's religious pictures painted for the Scolope Fathers of Madrid, in the Church of San Antonio. *Photo Mas, Barcelona*

119 THIS TERRIFYING PICTURE is one of the fourteen 'black paintings' that Goya painted as murals for his country house between 1819 and 1823. *Saturn* was painted as the main decoration in Goya's dining-room. It has since been transferred on to canvas and is in the Prado Museum, Madrid. *Photo Anderson*

119 TWO MEN FIGHTING WITH CLUBS, another of the 'black paintings'. They derived their name from the fact that they are all painted in dark colours, black and grey predominating, in stark contrast to most of his other paintings, full of colour and light. Prado Museum, Madrid. *Photo Mas, Barcelona*

120-1 THE PILGRIMAGE TO THE FOUNTAIN OF SAN ISIDRO is another of Goya's murals. It is interesting to compare this panoramic composition with the earlier *Pilgrimage of San Isidro* (page 62), to see how different Goya's treatment of the theme had become. The first is full of light and gaiety, the later one has a dark, sinister, and mocking quality. Prado Museum, Madrid. *Photo Anderson*

122 IT WAS MAINLY IN BORDEAUX, where he died, that Goya spent his last years. This engraving of 1828 shows part of the wide, well-laid-out streets of the city, near the sea-port. *Radio Times Hulton Picture Library*

123 DON RAMON SATUÉ is one of Goya's latest and finest portraits. It was painted in 1823. Don Ramon was an official of the Court at the time. *Photo by courtesy of the Rijksmuseum, Amsterdam*

124*THE MILKMAID OF BORDEAUX. This beautiful portrait is one of Goya's very last paintings, and shows his technique at its most advanced. It was painted at Bordeaux in 1827, a year before his death. It was later sold by his companion, Doña Leocadia Zorrilla Weiss, who declared that Goya had instructed her not to part with it for less than a gold *onza* (a Spanish coin worth about four pounds). Prado Museum, Madrid.

125 A DETAIL, showing Goya's signature, from a portrait of Don Manuel Osorio de Zuñiga. *Photo by courtesy of the Metropolitan Museum of Art, New York*

127 THIS PORTRAIT of Goya, at the age of eighty, was painted by Vicente Lopez y Portana, by order of King Ferdinand VII, in 1826, when Goya paid his last visit to Madrid. Prado Museum, Madrid. *Photo Mas, Barcelona*

128 GOYA'S TOMB in the cemetery at Bordeaux, where he died in April 1828 at the age of eighty-two. From Charles Yriarte's *Goya*, Paris, 1867. *By courtesy of the Trustees of the British Museum. Photo Thames and Hudson Archives*

INDEX OF NAMES

Page numbers in italics refer to pictures